Miller's book does not just advocate a "role" for women in the Church. As the title indicates, she explains what *authority* women already have. This is not a polemical or apologetic work but one that engages feminist theology with a wonderfully creative, deeply theological and biblically-based explanation of what authority means and how female authority differs from, yet is in relation to, male authority.

JANET E. SMITH

Professor of moral theology and the Fr. Michael J. McGivney Chair of Life Issues at the Sacred Heart Major Seminary in Detroit

This book is not what you expect. It is not what you've read before. It is an eye-opener for the importance of the question; for defining a clear alternative to androcentrism (male chauvinism), feminist fundamentalism, and a lukewarm compromise between them; and for a profoundly scriptural view of authority—one of the most disastrously misunderstood concepts in our culture.

PETER KREEFT

Author and Professor of philosophy at Boston College

A full-throated "thank you" to Monica Miller for this sublime response to Pope Francis' call for further development of our theology of woman. It would be a mistake to pigeonhole this work as a mere rejoinder to the demand for women priests. No, Miller has done her homework, gathering from Scripture, Tradition, Liturgy, the saints, Church Fathers, while at the same time showing she knows the arguments of radical feminist thought. Miller provides the fullest and clearest explanation—*and redemption*—of authority that I have ever read. Once Miller rescues authority from the banal distortion of the wielding of power and returns it to its true context of covenant and

D0006574

nuptial communion, it is not only the ministerial priesthood that is better understood *but the entire Christian faith.*

Executive Director of Theology of the Body Institute

Miller cuts through the angry façade of the women's rights movement to define true femininity, designed by God, as revealed through the Catholic Church. After four decades in the often-brutal pro-life trenches and as a college professor, Miller can stand shoulder-to-shoulder with any activist. She is perfectly suited to write about the authentic empowerment of women and provides a theology here that can heal a generation that has lost its way.

PATTI ARMSTRONG

Catholic author and speaker

Perhaps at no other time in the history of the Church has there been a greater need for a clear, cogent understanding of the authority of the female person and from whence it derives. In her work, Dr. Monica Migliorino Miller cuts through the chimera put forth by the culture of the day and reveals the source of woman's influence, effect, and power, and why woman can "aid humanity in not falling" and "save the peace of the world." A challenging, hard-hitting, and completely liberating study of the authority of woman!

JOHNNETTE S. BENKOVIC

Founder of Women of Grace and EWTN host

THE
AUTHORITY OF WOMEN
IN THE CATHOLIC CHURCH

THE
AUTHORITY OF WOMEN
IN THE CATHOLIC CHURCH

MONICA MIGLIORINO MILLER

EMMAUS
ROAD
PUBLISHING

Steubenville, Ohio
www.emmausroad.org

Emmaus Road Publishing
1168 Parkview Circle
Steubenville, Ohio 43952

Library of Congress Control Number: 2015938389
ISBN: 978-1-941447-15-4

Cover design by Mairead Cameron

For Fr. Donald Keefe, S.J. — from whom I learned everything

TABLE OF CONTENTS

FOREWORD

Every age is defined—at least in the history books—by the public conversations that occupy its intellectual classes. In one age it was the debates about labor and capital. In another it was the passionate exchange about the nature of governance. In still another it was about the relationship between religion and citizenship.

Can anyone doubt that the defining public conversation of our time is over the meaning of gender? Certainly it is so. With the sexual revolution, all the traditional roles and rules were overturned; and today our media and our courts are preoccupied with the fallout.

If the public exchange were a true conversation, it might be salutary. It might be good for us. But it's not. It's more like an exchange of gunfire. It's more like shots fired at long distance from behind bunkered walls. What should be reasoned out is instead flamed out in social-media comboxes, where everyone is raging and no one is listening.

How good it would be if we could move the exchange out of the battlefield, out of the comboxes, and even out of the courts.

This book is a beautiful beginning to a true conversation. Monica Miller is a voice of reason, charity, and wisdom. She is a scholar who has proven her *bona fides* in an activist life. She has never shied away from controversy. Yet she has never closed herself off from wide-ranging friendship. She genuinely listens to those who oppose her and those who disagree with her positions and she engages their objections. She comes forward with bold proposals, but she knows their boldness, and she is honestly testing them in the public forum.

I have known Dr. Miller for most of my adult life. We have not always agreed with one another, but I have always had profound respect for her courage and her willingness to take a conversation to the streets—to invite reflection and discussion. Again, that's what this book is all about.

Pope Francis has consistently expressed his desire for more discussion about the role of women in the Church. He has encouraged scholars to develop a more explicit language that can provide further insight into the feminine charism and how it is uniquely exercised within the Church and society. This discussion is certainly needed. The particular "genius of women"—their feminine participation in the covenantal relationship, their unique contribution to redemption, and how they concretely express their gifts in the Church—all of this is commonly misunderstood in the public dialogue and in the Church's own family.

The public discourse on the role of women in the Church often centers upon male ecclesial authority and frequently ends up challenging the faith and misconstruing the covenant of redemption between Christ and the Church. This book offers a positive proposal to explore more fully the covenantal, authoritative role women already have in the Catholic Church.

Secular authority often manifests itself through power. God expresses authority—not through quantitative force—but through life-giving force. When authority is correctly identified with the ability to give life and the responsibilities that are inherent in the creation of life, we begin to grasp the nature of male-female authority in the Catholic Church as it is presented in this book.

You'll find no novelties in this book. It is well grounded in the tradition. Those familiar with the Church's earliest centuries will find the seeds of Dr. Miller's ideas in the writings of St. Paul and the early Church Fathers, including Augustine, Jerome, Ambrose, John Chrysostom, and Cyprian. Feminine authority in the Catholic Church is not an abstract theory or a feel-good theology; it is a unique feminine responsibility for the faith that has been exercised—historically and concretely—in the lives of particular women, such as Judith, Deborah, Perpetua and Felicity, Monica, Catherine of Siena, and many heroic women of our own day.

In a 2004 letter to bishops on the Collaboration of Men and Women in the Church issued by the Congregation for the Doctrine of the Faith, Cardinal Joseph Ratzinger, prior to his election as Pope Benedict XVI, pointed us to the Paschal Mystery as the linchpin for understanding male and female complementary roles within the Church:

> Placed within Christ's Paschal mystery, they no longer see their difference as a source of discord to be overcome by denial or eradication, but rather as the possibility for collaboration, to be cultivated with mutual respect for their difference. From here, new perspectives open up for a deeper understanding of the dignity of women and their role in human society and in the Church.

May this book lead readers—and lead our public conversation—to "new perspectives" and a "deeper understanding" of the complementary gift the feminine charism is to the Catholic Church.

SCOTT HAHN

ABBREVIATIONS

PL. . . . . J.P. Migne, *Patrologia Latina*

PG . . . .J.P. Migne, *Patrologia Graeca*

CCL . . .*Corpus christianorum series latina*

CSEL. . *Corpus scriptorum ecclesiasticorum latinorum*

1
AUTHORITY
IN THE CATHOLIC CHURCH

In 1987 I attended a rally sponsored by the National Organization for Women (NOW). It took place in Denver on a warm day in June and was the climax of NOW's national conference. I had not, however, traveled to Denver to shake hands with Eleanor Smeal, who was then the president of NOW. Indeed, at the very same time this collection of radical feminists descended on the Colorado landscape, thousands of committed opponents of abortion had also arrived in the Rocky Mountain state for that year's National Right to Life Convention. A more real-time drama of the culture wars can hardly be imagined.

A small contingent of the more activist-oriented pro-lifers decided to counter-picket NOW's public gathering, and I counted myself among them. We hastily threw together some picket signs and waded into the crowd of militant feminists, flinging all caution to the wind. The goal of our tiny band of ten was simply to provide a witness to the injustice of abortion and, in some small measure, disrupt NOW's advocacy for a "woman's right to control her own body." We spread ourselves out to make our presence more effective and soon I found myself quite alone and isolated in a sea of angry pro-abortion women. Imprudently perhaps, I held my picket sign above my head and chanted pro-life slogans as loudly as I could in the hopes that at least someone nearby might pay attention to my message.

Someone certainly did and it happened to be a police officer. Within a matter of minutes I was placed under arrest, handcuffed, and escorted to a waiting police van. When I stumbled inside I saw that I was not alone. A few other handcuffed pro-lifers were already settled inside the van's dim interior. Apparently the Denver police felt a need to whisk us "troublemakers" off the street for fear that our vocal presence at the NOW rally would provoke a disturbance of the peace.

Within a matter of minutes I found myself incarcerated in a women's cellblock at the local Denver police station. I was actually placed in a private cell and thus for several hours I had no contact with anyone. Suddenly the door clanked open and a prison matron escorted me to a common area where other prisoners were seated. Dinner was about to be served. I found an open seat at a table occupied by three other women. We quickly got to talking. I explained my own predicament to them and found the three young women oddly friendly and sympathetic. I started to notice something about them—something that unnerved me. All three of them were bruised and two of them had whole sections of their scalps exposed. I could not fathom why they were so physically banged up. As I chewed on something that tasted like turkey I looked intently at the woman seated closest to me, a brunette in her early thirties, one of the women who had that strangely exposed scalp. Trying to sound nonchalant I asked, "What happened to your hair?" She looked me straight in the eye and said, "Oh, my boyfriend pulled it out."

I looked at this woman with an expression of shock. Indeed I was in shock. Suddenly everything about these women became sadly clear. Seated with me at this table in a prison were victims of domestic violence. A terrible dark world had just opened in front of me. Impulsively and naively I asked the women: "Why do you let men do this to you?"

"Well, sometimes we just get into it," came an answer from a blonde across the table.

Her response really meant, "This is just the way it is. This kind of violence between men and women is just expected. It's our way of life and we don't know anything different."

I continued my line of naive questions: "Well, why don't you leave these boyfriends?" The brunette seated closest to me whose boyfriend had yanked out her hair explained: "Where are we supposed to go? We have no jobs, we have no money, and I have kids with him."

More of that dark world opened up in front of me. These women expected to be abused and they were trapped—or at least they believed that they were trapped. I had, of course, known before that day that domestic violence existed but, as a consequence of getting arrested at a NOW rally, for the first time this dreadful reality was incarnated in front of me.

I found myself thrust between two perverted worlds. I had just left the world of committed NOW members militantly crusading for power that separates them from men in a radical individualism and isolation, enshrined in the slogan: "I have a right to do what I want with my own body." In jail I encountered the other world—the world where women have no respect at all, where indeed they do not have a "right to do what they want with their own body," where their bodies are abused by men who exploit and abuse them, and from whom they see little hope of escape. The radical feminist world that idolizes individual power and the right to self-determination believes it will liberate the women of the other world and enable such abused women to rise up and throw off the shackles of male dominance. But, in the end, the feminist extremists fail to free women because their campaign against the "war on women" is based on a false view of power, a false view of what it means to be human, a false view of what it means to be female. And indeed, how ironic that the woman who protested the NOW view of liberation and got herself arrested for it was the one who shared a prison dinner with women who were so desperately in need of finding and living the truth of their feminine authority.

However, it is not only the secular world that is steeped in confusion on the dignity and authority of women. The Catholic Church has been beset with such confusion for decades, a confusion fueled by the world's idea of power wherein many members in the Church base their view of women's liberation upon secular, wholly non-Christian sources offered by such groups as the National Organization for Women.

The majority of Catholics, and I would venture to say most people in general, believe that women in the Catholic Church do not possess any real power or authority. Feminists certainly believe this is true—and they want to change the situation. But this belief is shared even by very devout Catholics, except they believe the subordinate position of women is actually ordained by God and it is simply up to women to obey Him in this regard.

CALLING FOR A NEW THEOLOGY

Some years ago I told a nun whom I had met on retreat that I wished to write a book on the authority of women in the Catholic Church. Her response was, "Well, that'll be a short book!" Her statement was based on her view that as long as women are banned from becoming priests, and thus have no hierarchical position, they have no real ecclesial authority. That women cannot be ordained remains an issue of controversy and contention. The role of women in the Church is often centered on the fact that women may not be ordained to the priesthood.

St. Pope John Paul II definitively affirmed the Church's ban on women priests in his 1994 Apostolic Letter *Ordinatio Sacerdotalis:*

Wherefore, in order that all doubt may be removed regarding a matter of great importance, a matter which pertains to the Church's divine constitution itself, in virtue of my ministry of confirming the brethren (cf. Lk 22:32) I declare that the Church has no authority whatsoever to confer priestly ordination on women and that this judgment is to be definitively held by all the Church's faithful.

As recently as 2013, Pope Francis publicly reiterated that the Catholic Church cannot and will not ordain women to the ministerial priesthood. He even stated this to be the case in his first encyclical *Evangelii Gaudium*, no. 104: "The reservation of the priesthood to males, as a sign of Christ the Spouse who gives himself in the Eucharist, is not a question open to discussion. . . ."

The Church has been in a state of crisis over the role of women for a very long time. Despite the fact that the Catholic position regarding the all-male priesthood is formally settled on a doctrinal level, signs both inside and outside the Church indicate that conflict and confusion on the position of women in the Church is far from over. What is desperately needed is a true theology of feminine authority—indeed a true Catholic feminism. Pope Francis called for just such a theology in his September 30, 2013 *America Magazine* interview:

We must therefore investigate further the role of women in the Church. We have to work harder to develop a profound theology of the woman. Only by making this step will it be possible to better reflect on their function within the Church. The feminine genius is needed wherever we make important decisions. The challenge today is this: to think about the specific place of women also in those places where the authority of the Church is exercised for various areas of the Church.

This book intends to meet the pope's request and provide the reader with that theology of women so desperately needed in the Church today.

RECENT HISTORY OF WOMEN'S ORDINATION

On July 14, 2014, the General Synod of the Church of England under the authority of Justin Welby, Archbishop of Canterbury, voted to admit female bishops for the first time in its history. This measure may be considered the climax to a decades-long development within the Anglican and Episcopal Churches. In 1992, the Church of England, after a twenty year debate, voted to allow women priests. *Time* magazine dubbed this event the "Second Reformation." A week later the American Catholic bishops were unable to pass a controversial pastoral statement on women that had been in the works for nine years. The vote marked the first time since the National Conference of Catholic Bishops was formed in 1966 (now the USCCB) that the American bishops failed to reach a two-thirds majority needed to approve a proposed pastoral statement. Failure to gain the necessary votes lay in the complete lack of agreement even among bishops, not only on how to approach women's issues, but on what those issues even were. And, of course, there were bishops who would not endorse the document because it did not go far enough in affirming the feminist agenda. Soon after the failed vote on the pastoral statement, Archbishop Rembert Weakland, a retired bishop of Milwaukee sympathetic to the ordination of women, told a female audience at Trinity College that the debate over women's role in the Church and society "is not over, it's just starting."

Perhaps the debate has just begun. But the task of the loyal theologian is to provide thinking that is persuasive and creative in explaining the truth of the faith. The crisis before us demands this task. Many in the Church who classify themselves as feminists are committed to undoing the sacramental order of the Church, and most likely will not be persuaded by any argument no matter how intelligent or well articulated. But there are many more Catholics who desperately want to understand Church teaching and be faithful to it—Catholics who seek an *authentic Catholic feminism*. They are eager for reasons, a fresh perspective, and a coherent theology that explains the faith. Theological tools are needed to solve the crisis of faith that plagues Catholicism today.

The crisis concerning the role of women in the Church is no trifling or isolated matter. This question profoundly affects almost every aspect of ecclesial life: sacramental, liturgical, spiritual, and moral. Fundamentally, the crisis has to do with the meaning of authority itself. Women do possess authority in the Catholic Church. But if we think authority is synonymous with the holding of formal office, if it is strictly identified with juridical, legal, and political status, then this might very well be a short book. The task before us is to penetrate the true meaning of authority which, according to the Christian dispensation and the sacramental structure of the Church, has very little to do with such things. Let me repeat: women possess authority in the Catholic Church.

Edith Stein, the great German philosopher and Catholic martyr stated: "Woman . . . is called upon to embody in her highest and purest development the essence of the Church—to be its symbol."[1] Women, and not men, exemplify the Church. For the purposes of understanding feminine authority and the covenant of redemption itself, this exemplification cannot be overemphasized. The authority of women is different from the authority exercised by the Catholic ordained priesthood. However, it is an authority complementary to the priesthood and it is an authority without which the sacramental life of the Church and redemption, itself, would not exist. The

---

1. Edith Stein, *The Collected Works of Edith Stein,* Vol. 2: Essays on Women, ed. Dr. L. Gebler and Romaeus Leuven (Washington, D.C.: ICS Publications, 1987), 230.

authority of woman as Mother Church—Mater Ecclesia—is so pre-rational, so close to us, and perhaps most importantly, by its own nature, un-enshrined by sacramental office so that it easily goes un-noticed and is misunderstood.

Contemporary critics of the Church, particularly those who classify themselves as feminist theologians, believe the hierarchical structure of all-male priestly authority is an inherently unjust system and sinful in its exclusion of women from positions of power. Their attack is based upon a secular view of authority as a quantifiable force, exercised visibly and publicly by persons who hold a special position or office. So feminists conclude that those who do not pos-sess public office have no authority—at least none that is significant outside of, perhaps, the right to vote. Since women are denied access to Church office, it must be obvious to all that they, ipso facto, are without power. Feminist theologians, especially, believe that women in relation to the hierarchical priesthood are in a position of subjec-tion because they are not permitted to share in this formal, visible office. Women thus cannot speak, cannot direct anyone, and cannot set Church policies. Because men alone, so it seems, are in a ruling and teaching position, feminists resent that their destinies are bound to the directives of men. Elizabeth Johnson, one of the most influ-ential feminist theologians working today, articulates the feminist complaint against the Church very clearly. In her book *She Who Is: The Mystery of God in Feminist Theological Discourse* she writes:

> Conversely [women] have been depersonalized as a roman-tic, unsexed ideal whose fulfillment lies mainly in mother-hood. Even as I write, women in the Catholic community are excluded from full participation in the sacramental sys-tem, from ecclesial centers of significant decision making, law making and symbol making and from official public leadership roles whether in governance or the liturgical

assembly. They are called to honor a male savior sent by a male God whose legitimate representatives can only be male, all of which places their persons precisely as female in a peripheral role. Their femaleness is judged to be not suitable as a metaphor for speech about God. In a word, women occupy a marginal place in the official life of the church, that is, necessarily there but of restricted value.[2]

As this book will show, Johnson's complaint is based on a mistaken view of the covenant of redemption. Most theologians who share her view believe that the only way for women to achieve recognition and power is for them to be associated with the power of God Himself, and if they cannot serve as a "suitable metaphor" for God then they believe the feminine role is less valued when compared to men and especially male priests. The problem with this view is that it does not actually value what is particular and unique to the role of women in the Church, because for such thinkers it is only God's voice that matters, and everyone should be speaking His part to have any worth in the covenant of redemption.

Fundamentally, the current crisis of authority concerning the position of women in the Church has to do with how Christians understand the order of redemption itself. This order of redemption has to do with how salvation is actually communicated to the world. How is Jesus in relation to His Church? The crisis of women and authority affects the very identity of the Christian people because it strikes at the very heart of the structure of the Catholic Church and her worship. This crisis troubles the faith-life of Christians, particularly in the areas of morality and the sacraments.

---

2. Elizabeth A. Johnson, *She Who Is: The Mystery of God in Feminist Theological Discourse* (New York: The Crossroad Publishing Company,1993), 26.

THE MEANING OF AUTHORITY

The crisis can only really be resolved when Christians come to appreciate that real authority is not synonymous with power. The person who possesses authority is not simply or always the strong one within a group who then uses his strength to organize the group around his vision. Someone who has this power can declare himself outside the group and exert a dominant position towards the group in a world in which there is no inherent relation between the leader and the group. Nor is there any real relation among any of the members of the group. In fact, if order is achieved by the wielding of power, this presupposes that the group has no meaning or purpose outside of the leader's will. Dictators and tyrants know this better than anyone. This is the Nietzcheian world without ontological truth or harmony, but this is not the world of God the Father. God has not created a world in which authority is arbitrary and a mere matter of quantifiable strength. In other words, we need to get away from the idea that whoever holds office, whoever has the most strength of will, whoever has strength because of size or numbers is the one who therefore has authority or is deserving of respect. Catholics do not respect or look up to their priests simply because they are nice guys or great moral leaders. Priests are respected because of whom they represent and for whom they are a living sacrament. Namely, a priest manifests the authority of Christ, as Jesus is the Eucharistic life-giver to His Church.

The question needs to be asked: Why should anyone obey God? In what way does God have authority that calls for man's obedience? If we were to take a poll on this question there would undoubtedly be several answers. For instance, perhaps God should be obeyed because He is almighty in the sense that He can wipe people out if they do not listen to Him or punish them for disobedience. In other words, God is obeyed precisely because He has raw power. Or perhaps God should be obeyed because He is the law-giver, and justice demands that if human beings transgress what He has decreed, punishment is in order. After all, God is the Supreme Being, superior to man in every way, and He therefore has the right to demand that we listen to Him.

But if we really want to understand God's authority and thus any real authority, whether exercised by God or man, we need to take a look at the action of God in history. God's action towards the human race provides the foundation of our obedience to Him. Also, simply a look at the word *authority* itself will be helpful.

The word *authority* comes from the Latin *auctores*, meaning "to be the author or creator of something." A person has authority precisely by giving life. If God has authority, it is because He is life itself and the Creator of all life. When Christians recite the Nicene Creed, the first item of faith declared is, "I believe in God, the Father the Almighty, the maker of heaven and earth." Yes, God is "the Almighty," but not in the sense of simply holding power over something in some arbitrary way. Rather, "maker of heaven and earth" defines the almighty character of God. He is truly almighty because He alone can create out of nothing. The fact that He does create is the essence of God's authority.

The Book of Exodus tells the story of how God creates for Himself a people, the Chosen People. Yahweh establishes a covenant with the Hebrew people, a covenant requiring obedience to the ordinances of God, not simply because God demands obedience for its own sake, but because obedience to God brings life to the Hebrews. It is precisely this obedience to God's moral code that marks the Jews as a people chosen by Him.

> "For this commandment which I command you this day is not too hard for you, neither is it too far off. . . . See, I have set before you this day life and good, death and evil. If you obey the commandments of the Lord your God which

I command you this day, by loving the Lord your God, by
walking in his ways, and by keeping his commandments
and his statutes and his ordinances, then you shall live and
multiply, and the Lord your God will bless you in the land
which you are entering to take possession of it. But if your
heart turns away, and you will not hear, but are drawn away
to worship other gods and serve them, I declare to you this
day, that you shall perish; you shall not live long in the land
which you are going over the Jordan to enter and possess. I
call heaven and earth to witness against you this day, that I
have set before you life and death, blessing and curse; therefore choose life, that you and your descendants may live,
loving the Lord your God, obeying his voice and clinging to
him." (Deut 30:11, 15–20)

Life and prosperity is clearly connected with love of God and
obedience to Him. The Jews will not have a long life in the land
they are crossing the Jordon to occupy if they fail to follow God.
Obedience to God is not an arbitrary thing but is connected to life.
This is clearly the lesson of Genesis. Adam and Eve, because of their
disobedience, did not enjoy a "long life" in Eden. They wished to be
"like gods" themselves and so disobeyed the one true God. Their disobedience, their sin, brought death to themselves and to the whole
world. If they had recognized God's authority, they would have recognized His authority was connected to His having given them life.

Why should God be obeyed? Because He is the source of life.
Obedience to God keeps man alive by keeping him connected to
his source of life. Simple fear can motivate obedience to God, but if
God has given the gift of life, then obedience can easily be motivated
by love. And, of course, this is the ideal. But to disobey God brings
death. After all, real death, the death of hell, is separation from God.

Obedience to God allows the human being to live and know the source of life and human freedom. Authority is the power to give life, but equally as important, authority is entirely bound up with the rights and responsibilities that are connected to this power so that the life that has been brought forth may come to its proper fulfillment. This is the proper definition of authority. God requires man's obedience, not because God is a megalomaniac or egomaniac, but so that man, who is utterly dependent upon God's creative action, may maintain his dignity as a creature of a loving God and come to his proper fulfillment. In a sense, if God creates, He is "responsible" for the well-being of this creation, and to require the human being's obedience is not simply God's prerogative and right, but is something bound up with God's care for His creation.

Bound up with God's creative will is the beauty and also the horror of human freedom. We can say no. If God is not a despot creator, a power that imposes itself as a foreigner from the outside unrelated to His creation, then He had to let man be free. This freedom between God and man is the essence of the covenant. Man freely enters into union with God. This unity, if it is true, must be unforced. Any love affair requires this freedom.

AUTHORITY AND THE COVENANT

If authority is the power to give life and the responsibility to oversee the good for that life, then it is not too hard to understand Christ's authority in relation to the Church. The first principle of Christ's authority is that it exists within a covenant. Authority is covenantal. Christ is actually in union with that to which He exercises authority—namely the Church. There is a love relation between Christ and that over which He exercises authority.

Ultimately, authority can only be properly understood by first looking at the Trinity. The Trinity is three distinct persons within one single Godhead who are in relation to one another. Indeed, it is their relationality that defines them. For example, it is the Father who begets the Son. Language, of course, always falters in the face of this greatest mystery, but one can say that, in a true sense, these Persons of the Trinity are dependent upon one another. Again, it is the Father who begets the Son, and it is the Holy Spirit who proceeds from the Father and the Son. The Father, the First Person of the Trinity, would not be Father were it not for the Second Person, and the Second Person, different from the First and different from the Holy Spirit, cannot occupy their place. Notice also, that in the economy of salvation, it is the Son who is sent by the Father to save the world from sin, yet Christ's divinity and dignity are no less than that of the Father. But they are different. This difference however does not render one less than the other.

It is even possible to say that the Son is subordinate to the Father, again in the sense that He is sent by the Father. Christ is also subordinate, as the Gospels affirm many times, because Christ does only what the Father tells Him (see for example Jn 5:19, 30; 14:10). Christ's work is dependent on the Father. Christ does not consider this a threat to His dignity but rather the fulfillment of it. Even the Lord of Lords and the King of Kings was obedient! Certainly, this is the lesson of Gethsemane. There Christ cried out: "Not my will, but yours, be done" (Lk 22:42).

The exercise of true authority is done *in relation*. Pope Benedict XVI has done some insightful thinking on the relations of the Persons in the Trinity that is helpful for understanding the true meaning of authority. In God there is unity and oneness, but also plurality. The Christian teaching on the oneness and yet plurality of God truly sets this religion apart from all others. Plurality is not disintegration as many believe. Benedict XVI teaches that plurality is not the result of an antagonistic dualism of powers.

The Trinity shows that the highest unity is not the lonely, indivisible one, the isolated monad that is completely unrelated to anything. Or as Benedict says, unity is not "the indivisibility of the atom, the smallest unity, too small to be divided up; the authentic acme of unity is the unity created by love. The multi-unity which grows in love is a more radical, truer unity than the unity of the 'atom.'"[3]

This unity "created by love" sets up a dialogue which is possible only because there is differentiation.

Authority, if it has any basis in the truth of the oneness and plurality of the Trinity, is not some single thing. God Himself is not some single atomistic thing without relation, and neither is the Church and the authority that functions within her. Authority exists in a covenant—indeed, in a free dialogue between Christ and the Church.

The fundamental salvific action of Christ established a covenant. The New Covenant was created through the very blood of Christ poured out on the Cross. The Eucharist itself makes this truth present as the words of Christ at the Last Supper proclaim: "Drink of it, all of you, for this is my blood of the covenant, which is poured out for many for the forgiveness of sins" (Mt 26:27–28).

The covenant is not between Christ and Himself; it is between Christ and something *other* than Himself—His people baptized into His Body, His Church. The covenant of salvation is made up of two entities joined in an intimate and unbreakable union. The authority of Christ serves this union. He is the life-giver to this Body. And so priests stand in the place of this life-giver. But the Church too has an authority. Women are the proper symbol and manifestation of it. If feminine authority is to be properly understood it must be understood in the inherent sacramental relation: the relation not between women and the priesthood, but between women and the Church.

---

3. Joseph Cardinal Ratzinger, *Introduction to Christianity* (New York: Herder and Herder, 1969), 128.

MARRIAGE AND THE COVENANT

The covenantal nature of the authority of Christ and the Church means that we are staring the reality of marriage in the face. The authority of this New Covenant is not only the authority of bishops and priests, an authority held by men who through Holy Orders stand in the place of Christ. The New Covenant is the marital union between Christ and the Church, so even the meaning of Church authority is marital. In 1976, the Vatican issued a document called *Inter Insigniores* or "Declaration on the Question of Admission of Women to the Ministerial Priesthood." It teaches that the covenant, even from Old Testament times, had a nuptial character. The Chosen People are the spouse of God. The New Covenant is founded by the blood of Christ, the New Adam:

> From his pierced side will be born the Church, as Eve was born from Adam's side. At that time there is fully and eternally accomplished the nuptial mystery proclaimed and hymned in the Old Testament: Christ is the Bridegroom; the Church is his Bride, whom he loves because he has gained her by his blood and made her glorious, holy and without blemish, and henceforth he is inseparable from her.[4]

Remarkably, the document then states: "That is why we can never ignore the fact that Christ is a man." This is an important statement. It is obvious that *Inter Insigniores* considers Christ's masculinity significant. The document teaches something even shocking when it not only affirms that Christ came as a male, but when, in defense of the male priesthood, it goes on to say: "Christ Himself was and remains a man." The word *man* in the original Latin text is not

---

4. Sacred Congregation for the Doctrine of the Faith, Declaration on Women to the Ministerial Priesthood *Inter Insigniores* (October 15, 1976) in *Vatican Council II: More Post Conciliar Documents*, Vol. 2, ed. Austin Flannery, O.P. (Collegeville, MN: The Liturgical Press, 1982), 340.

simply *human* but *vir,* meaning "male" (*Christus ipse fuit et permanet vir*). The believer needs to deal with this. The document declares that *even now,* even in Christ's glorified, heavenly existence, due to the Incarnation, Jesus is male. In other words, Jesus is now and forever a guy! This is so according to the unity of the Divine Son of God with the male gender in the conception of Christ in the womb of Mary. Jesus does not shed His body, but His body and thus his male human sexuality is forever within the mystery of the Godhead united to His person. A more radical doctrinal statement on the meaning of masculinity can hardly be imagined. The statement is rather shocking and drives home the point that an inherent relation exists between the Person of Christ and the male priest who sacramentally signs Christ to the Church.

The eternal masculinity of Christ reveals that the significance of gender is not simply on some biological level, but actually significant to salvation itself. By it Christ establishes the marital character of the New Covenant. This also means that the marital character is not just one metaphor among others. It is not just one way of looking at the order of redemption. Rather, because Christ's sexual gender has meaning, sexuality as such is part and parcel of the economy of salvation. In light of certain feminist challenges to the faith, there is a desperate and even urgent need to understand just how the female sex is equally indispensable to the New Covenant. We need to become conscious of how feminine authority complements the masculinity of Christ and the ordained priesthood.

The most common support for the all-male priesthood is that this has always been the tradition of the Church. Even *Inter Insigniores* emphasized this argument. Christ called no women to be Apostles, and the Church has an unbroken practice of ordaining only men. The unbroken practice, based upon the action of the Lord Himself, is an indication to the Church of the will of God in the matter. This is a weighty argument but in some ways it is not the most fruitful in terms of getting to the heart of why authority is differentiated between men and women in the Church. The most fertile theological ground lies in understanding the relationship between sexuality and the covenant, and between sexuality and the sacraments. However, even taking this approach is something of an uphill battle. Years ago Archbishop Weakland, commenting on women's ordination, stated that many theologians and faithful Catholics have attempted to use the symbolic relation between Christ and the Church to explain why women cannot be priests, "but in a most unconvincing way."[5]

There are a number of reasons why Catholics are not convinced by this argument. First, most priests, bishops, theologians, and catechists do not promote it. But there is probably a deeper reason why Catholics and the larger public are unconvinced that anything is at stake if women were to be ordained. Modern culture has lost its appreciation for the importance of symbols. American society, for the most part, believes that symbols are arbitrary, that they are simply human constructs and thus purely conventional—even religious symbols. Moreover, our society, and indeed nearly all of Western European culture, no longer believes that sexuality, sexual behavior, and even marriage have any inherent meaning. The growing acceptance of same-sex marriage is a sure indication that our culture is forfeiting any belief that male and female sexuality has inherent meaning. The progress of the gay rights movement is staggering. Sex and sexuality are now only what a person believes them to be. Intercourse has no meaning outside of a person's subjective feelings about it. Intercourse certainly is no longer considered to have an exclusively marital meaning. Non-marital intercourse is almost universally accepted and treated as a matter of fact.

In other words, gender and sexual activity now stand outside of the realm of absolutes. This is clear when even homosexual "mar-

5. Archbishop Rembert Weakland, "Weakland Questions Male-Only Priesthood," *Milwaukee Sentinel*, Oct. 23, 1992, 8.

riages" are taken seriously, when such unions are codified by law and homosexuals thus granted the same marital status and privileges as heterosexuals. At this point we can only stand back in amazement and wonder what, if anything, do gender and sexual activity mean? With so much confusion concerning sexual matters abounding everywhere, it is no wonder that people are unable to appreciate that a relation exists between human sexuality and sacraments.

The Pharisees challenged Jesus on the question of divorce in an attempt to trip Him up. Christ answered them by going back to the Beginning, namely to the Book of Genesis (Mt 19: 3–9; Mk 10:2–12). We must also go back to the Beginning to find the foundation for the relation between sexuality and sacraments. Genesis declares, "It is not good that the man should be alone" (2:18). So God created the woman, the "suitable partner." The passage is well known:

> So the Lord God caused a deep sleep to fall upon the man, and while he slept took one of his ribs and closed up its place with flesh; and the rib which the Lord God had taken from the man he made into a woman and brought her to the man. Then the man said, "This at last is bone of my bones and flesh of my flesh; she shall be called Woman, because she was taken out of Man." Therefore a man leaves his father and his mother and clings to his wife, and they become one flesh. (Gen 2:21–24)

This most beautiful passage is theologically very rich. These verses confront us with the essence of human existence. But not only this, we have to wait until the revelation of the New Testament for the full disclosure of truth about marriage and human sexuality. This is found most specifically in Ephesians 5:22–32. If there is anything that demonstrates once and for all that human sexuality has meaning beyond the mere biological level, it is the fact that the very same verses from Genesis are found in Ephesians 5. St. Paul does something remarkable. He provides a treatise on the relation between marriage and Christ's unity with the Church that is climaxed specifically with the quotation from Genesis 2:24:

> As the Church is subject to Christ, so let wives also be subject in everything to their husbands. Husbands, love your wives, as Christ loved the Church and gave himself up for her, that he might sanctify her, having cleansed her by the washing of water with the word, that he might present the Church to himself in splendor, without spot or wrinkle or any such thing, that she might be holy and without blemish. Even so husbands should love their wives as their own bodies. He who loves his wife loves himself. For no man ever hates his own flesh, but nourishes and cherishes it, as Christ does the Church, because we are members of his body. "For this reason a man shall leave his father and mother and be joined to his wife, and the two shall become one flesh." This is a great mystery, and I mean in reference to Christ and the Church. (Eph 5:24–32)

What is the great mystery? To what, precisely, does the word *this* in verse 32 refer? The "this" is the marital bond of the first man and the first woman. Their one-flesh marital union from the very beginning of time is the sign of Christ and the Church. The one-flesh unity is not a mere metaphor or poetry as if sexuality was only a temporary symbol that could be replaced if only we could find some better way to express the unity between the Church and Christ. The fact is, there is no better way! There is nothing better. There is only something better if the very meaning of creation and marriage can be undone! But the meaning of creation and marriage is given by God in the Beginning. When Ephesians quotes Genesis 2:24 on the original unity of man and woman and then states that this refers to "Christ and the Church," the meaning of sexuality is revealed here. Man and woman are the original sacraments of the New Covenant; their conjugal love is a prophecy for Christ and the Church.

If man and woman are the original sacraments, this means that their roles cannot be blurred, cannot overlap, and cannot be exchanged. Not only creation, but as Ephesians testifies, redemption also is filled with marital meaning. This has important implications for the meaning of Church authority. It too exists according to a nuptial pattern. Christ is the Head of the Church because He is her spouse. The Church is His Bride because she is His Body—in the most intimate and indissoluble way. Christ has authority because He gives life as the Head, and He has responsibility for whom He has brought to life. But, again, salvation is made real and possible for the world through the covenant of Christ and the Church. And since this covenant exists nuptially, man and woman do not give life in the same way. If Christ's sexuality is to be taken seriously, then there must be something masculine about the way Christ gives life to the Church that in fact makes Him the Church's Head. If the Church's feminity is to be taken seriously, then there must be something feminine about the way the Church gives life in union with the Head that in fact makes her His Body. This means that the Church, in relation to Christ, possesses authority that is feminine in essence. According to the one-flesh union of Christ and the Church, authority is differentiated. A man and a woman give life together, and in ways that are complementary and fulfill one another. Each makes their life-giving and thus authoritative contribution, sexually delineated, which is the basis upon which the nuptial covenant is possible at all.

The extremist feminist solution to ecclesial authority erases differentiation between men and women, between God and matter, and between Christ and the Church. In feminist philosophy, peace, justice, and equality are achieved when everything is absorbed into the faceless, impersonal, monistic, platonic One. Such a view of authority demolishes the entire meaning of God's creation: God called something "good" that was differentiated from Himself (Gen 1). The New Covenant between Christ and the Church exists maritally and thus it is within the "one flesh" union of the New Adam and the New Eve that the authentic meaning of male and female authority is discovered. In his 1983 pastoral letter on the priesthood *Do This in Memory of Me*, the late Cardinal Emmett Carter of Toronto stated:

> [T]his sacrifice is that of the Head of the Body, offered for the Body. The Head-Body relation is marital, covenantal. In this relation, the authority-structure of the Trinity is imaged: the subsistent relations of the Father, Son and Spirit have their created analogue in the Head, the Body, the One Flesh of the New Covenant.
>
> As the persons who mutually constitute the Triune God are defined by their relatedness, as their authority is thereby qualified while remaining undiminished, wholly divine, so in the New Covenant the Head, the Body, and the One Flesh of their sacrificial union are constituted by their interrelation, and their mutual authority is qualitatively differentiated without subjection. The Head gives Himself totally to the Bridal Church who gives herself totally in reply and both are under the authority, the irrevocability, of their union in One Flesh.[6]

"Both are under the authority . . . of their union in One Flesh." This is the key to understanding the essence of authority. The authority of the Head and the authority of the Body are at the service of *their union*. The One-Flesh union establishes how authority is exercised and for what purpose. The authority of the Head or Body does not function except under the meaning of their unity. At this point authority is not arbitrary. It is not sheer strength of will; it is not simply the power to

---

6. G. Emmett Cardinal Carter, "Do this in memory of me": A Pastoral Letter Upon the Sacrament of Holy Orders (Toronto: Mission Press, 1983).

rule over others. The one-flesh unity has authority over the couple. The Head and the Body not only make up this unity, but they are bound by its meaning. And the Head and the Body lead each other to the fulfillment of that meaning. In a marriage, the authority of husband and wife is authentic when it brings that marriage to fulfillment. The nuptial structure of redemption determines what authority is in the Catholic Church. Ecclesiastical authority, as it is held by the pope, bishops, and priests, is fundamentally service. In other words, authority, rooted in the marital structure of the New Covenant, is responsibility for the faith. We are concerned about understanding this responsibility, particularly the responsibility of women.

If redemption is accomplished according to a marriage between Jesus and the Church, then male and female sexuality are the symbols of this covenant. The covenant is dependent on these symbols and would have no concrete historical expression without them. Since the New Covenant exists in the world according to a marital structure, responsibility for the faith, or authority, is differentiated according to the meaning of these sexual symbols. The authority of the male hierarchy exists over and against the feminine Church whose femininity is expressed in the concrete lives of Christian women. Men and women possess authority differentiated according to the manner in which they give life. To the extent that this differentiated responsibility becomes blurred, Christianity itself ceases to be effectively expressed. When the meaning of sexual symbols is undone, the Christian faith is undone. Authority is exercised according to a one-flesh union (the head and the body) in which the symbols affecting this union are not dissolved or confused but fulfilled.

Because the covenant of Christ is a marriage, women possess authority, according to the meaning of their own sexuality, in relation to the ministerial priesthood that is integral to the world's salvation in Christ. The authority of women exists in relation to, as the complement of, and over and against the masculine authority of the priesthood. Consistent with an authentic feminism, this feminine authority is equal to, but qualitatively different from, the ministerial priesthood.

Perhaps a look at the words of St. Paul will be helpful here. He expresses the meaning of male/female authority when he states: "Nevertheless, in the Lord woman is not independent of man nor man of woman; for as woman was made from man, so man is now born of woman. And all things are from God" (1 Cor 11:11–12). At once the passage affirms dependence and mutuality between man and woman; furthermore, their dependency and mutuality exists precisely according to the differentiated manner by which each one bestows life upon the other! In "the beginning" woman was from man as Eve came from the rib of Adam, but now all men are born from women and "all is of God." This means that both man and woman can claim that their life-giving abilities, which constitute their differentiated authority, come from the will of God.

The masculinity of Christ is fulfilled according to the model of the old Adam. Adam's authority exists in that he is the source of the woman, as Christ through the offering up of Himself is the source of the Church. This is the meaning of Christ's headship to the Church. He is the cause of the Church. But woman also exists as source. Woman, according to the meaning of her own sexuality, is a cause: "Man is now born of woman."

The authority of Christ as Head means that He is the source of the New People of God. But having received her being from the Head, the Church in turn makes it possible for Christ's redemption to be accomplished in the world. Even the Eucharistic worship of the Church expresses this truth. The Eucharist is the celebration of the one-flesh unity between Christ and the Church in which their roles are not blurred. Thus the symbols that effect this reality must also not be blurred. The meaning of the Catholic priesthood exists within the marital order of redemption, as the priest stands in the place of

Christ as He is the source of the Church's existence. And the meaning of Christ as source is inherently masculine. The male person is the appropriate sign of the way Christ gives life to the Church. If feminine authority is to be appreciated and put into practice, it is necessary to understand how women are the appropriate sign of the Church in relation to the male priesthood.

The Eucharist makes present the sacrifice of Christ for the Church, the sacrifice that is the cause of her being.[7] But the Church makes a covenantal response that is uniquely her own, a sacrifice of praise, which completes the Eucharist.[8] The society of Christ and the Church is at one with the Eucharistic sacrifice

> in which the Bridegroom gives Himself totally to and for his bridal Church in the freedom of his mission from the Father, and receives from his immaculate Bride that which is indispensable to the New Covenant, all that she, in her created and covenantal and immaculately free dignity, has to give: the nuptial Body of which he, by her self-giving, her "sacrifice of praise," is the nuptial head.[9]

The order of redemption is the "one flesh" of Christ, the Head, and His Body, the Church. The Christian comes into contact with this one-flesh unity of Christ and the Church through the Eucharistic celebration. If the New Covenant is maritally ordered, then the central worship of the Church is constituted by masculine and feminine symbols. The conjugal love of a man and woman is the fundamental liturgical expression of Christ's unity with His people.

---

7. Second Vatican Council, Dogmatic Constitution on the Church *Lumen Gentium* (November 21, 1964) in *The Conciliar and Post Conciliar Documents*, ed. Austin Flannery, O.P. (Costello Publishing Co.: Northport, NY, 1980), 359.

8. Ibid., 361.

9. Donald Keefe, S.J., "Gender, History, and Liturgy in the Catholic Church," *Review for Religious*, 46 (Nov.–Dec. 1987), 876.

Here in the Eucharist, Christ, the Head, and the Church, His Body, are one.

The authority of men and women in the Catholic Church serves to build up this expression. Authority, then, is first liturgical before it is ever juridical. Authority serves the Church's worship and, since the New Covenant is a marital dialog between Christ and His people, men and women in the Church do not speak the same parts. This is at once the reality of the covenant as well as its beauty.

2
THE FEMINIST DESTRUCTION
OF THE COVENANT

All that Caeli wanted to do was get a haircut, but she wound up getting an education she didn't expect. As a college student at Madonna
University, her finances were meager but she decided to spend a few
extra dollars and made an appointment at an upscale salon in down-
town Ann Arbor, Michigan. She arrived a little early. There was only
one other customer already in the middle of a getting a perm. Caeli
thought it was a little odd that this other customer was a man, since
the salon catered to a female clientele. She also thought it odd that
a man would be getting a perm. But hey, this was Ann Arbor, and
while not quite as diverse as say Berkeley or Madison, or
certainly Greenwich Village, Ann Arbor had its share of unconven-
tional personalities.

   As is not uncommon inside a beauty parlor, the man sitting in
the chair was engaged in friendly banter with his beautician. The
subject of conversation was his upcoming wedding, which he spoke
about with great enthusiasm and in a rather forced effeminate manner. Another hair stylist escorted Caeli to a chair right next to him.
She noticed he was wearing makeup and his eyebrows were plucked.
She came to a stereotyped conclusion that when this man talked of
marriage he meant "gay marriage." Caeli then noticed that on a coat
rack nearby there was a lovely white wedding dress and veil pro-
tected by a covering of plastic.

His beautician remarked, "That is one of the most beautiful wedding dresses I've ever seen. Did you just pick it up for your fiancé?"

"No sweetheart," the man said, "That's not for her. It's for me."

Caeli and the beautician at this point exchanged glances. Caeli turned to the man. "I've got to say I am kind of confused right now. The dress is for you?"

"Yes, dear. It's for me."

"Ok—but aren't you a guy?"

"Oh, we don't believe in those gender labels."

"So then you're both wearing dresses?"

"No. She's wearing a tux. I'm wearing a dress. We're doing something different. We're switching it up!"

"So you're taking the place of the bride and she's taking the place of the groom."

"We're taking the role—as you put it—with the gender with which we identify."

By now Caeli's head lathered with shampoo was spinning and all she could say at that point was, "Interesting." Though no one in the salon could tell, she was in a kind of shock, having been caught completely off guard by a whole new vision of the world in which male and female sexuality had been emptied of all objective meaning. She was totally unprepared for this vision. Same-sex marriage was one thing, but this? In what category did this kind of nuptials belong?

While feminist theology doesn't quite advocate that male and female roles are entirely interchangeable, it believes that men and women fundamentally can and ought to speak the same parts. In feminism, any differences between men and women are negligible and certainly have no religious significance. The most important element of feminist ideology is its horror of distinction. Distinctions are the cause of injustice. For example, injustice between men and women means that they do not, indeed cannot, share everything. Their relationships are always in conflict. One will have what the other does not and hold it against the other for not having it. The way to eliminate injustice is to eliminate distinctions. Justice will reign when everything and everyone is the same.

In feminism, not only are there no important distinctions between men and women, but much of radical feminist thought maintains there are no distinctions between Christ and the Church, between priests and laity, and even between God and the earth. In such feminism the Christian religion is essentially an egalitarian democracy in which everyone, in principle, has the same position and exercises the same authority.

From a feminist point of view, the chief evils of the world are things called "patriarchy" and "androcentrism" which give rise to inherently unjust hierarchical power structures because such structures permit only the few to possess power. In the Catholic Church, of course, these few are of the male sex only. Patriarchy comes from the Greek word *patria*, meaning "father." Feminists oppose patriarchy because they believe it is in itself an ethic of power that orders a society in such a way that all men have power over all women. Men, by virtue of their superiority, are the rulers and women the subjects. The patriarchal system of domination and subordination encompasses all sorts of evils: racism, classism, as well as sexism. It is even the cause of speciesism—the belief that man is superior to animals and that some animals have more value than others. Patriarchy is any system of power based on an intrinsic distinction between persons that results in those who rule and those who are subordinate to that rule.

Feminists believe that patriarchy is the result of androcentrism. The word *andro* also comes from the Greek meaning "man" or "male." Androcentrism is a male-centered view of the world based on the idea that the male person sums up what it means to be fully human: male work, male thinking, male accomplishments, male strength, etc., defines the world. In such a system of thought, the existence of women is justified only to the extent that they truly are the male helpers. Outside of helping men do their work, women have no significance. Feminists believe the Catholic hierarchy with its all-male priesthood is androcentric to its core, and uses its androcentrism to shore up its power base that keeps women in a state of subjugation.

That is a perverted view of the Catholic religion and the way authority is exercised within it. Authority in the Church, because it is the authority of a covenant, has nothing to do with subjugation. Authority has to do with giving life and taking responsibility for life which is maritally differentiated.

Feminists hope to correct the "unjust androcentric power structure of the Church" by moving from an androcentric interpretation of the world to a gynocentric interpretation.[1] Women's experience is the means of interpreting reality. The experience of women, that is to say, women who hold to the feminist perspective, is the most important factor in the formulation of feminist theology. Female physical experience, female talents, female oppression, female feelings, female contributions, female thought, etc., are the filters through which all reality is judged—including the revelation of God. Consider this quote from Elisabeth Schüssler Fiorenza, one of the leading feminist biblical scholars:

> The locus or place of divine revelation is therefore not the Bible or the tradition of a patriarchal church but the *ekklesia* of women and the lives of women who live the "option of our women's selves." It is not simply the "experience of women" but the experience of women . . . from patriarchal oppression.[2]

---

1. Elisabeth Schüssler Fiorenza, *In Memory of Her*, (New York: Crossroad, 1983), xx–xxi.

2. Elisabeth Schüssler Fiorenza, "The Will to Choose or Reject: Continuing Our Critical Work" in *Feminist Interpretation of the Bible*, ed. by L. Russell (Oxford: Basil Blackwell, 1985), 128.

In terms of the Judeo-Christian religion, this approach to reality is quite a revolution. Indeed, it is basically incompatible with Judaism and Christianity. While human experience is important and not to be ignored, the Judeo-Christian religion does not derive its truth and authority from such experience. Rather, the Judeo-Christian religion is a revealed religion. God entered human history from the outside. His word spoken to man is something utterly new and cannot be accounted for by human experience. Feminists reject this idea. If God entered human history from the outside, as a God facing His creation, this means God is wholly different from nature. The feminist has a horror of this kind of distinction.

The radically feminist theological perspective believes that the concept of revealed religion is itself the result of androcentrism. Indeed, the late Mary Daly, one of the most radical of the radical feminists, even went so far as to claim that dating back five thousand years every major world religion is the result of an oppressive patriarchal order with not a single truth worth preserving among them. The only answer is to simply start over from a completely feminine viewpoint. Revealed religion is especially corrupt since it props up a masculine view of reality. God is distinct from nature and is its Lord and Master. If the dignity of human beings is to be respected, particularly the dignity of women, the Christian religion must be corrected by feminism. However, this move from a supposedly androcentric faith to a feminist one is not a correction but a manipulation of faith. The whole Christian religion would have to be altered in terms of who Christ is, the sacraments, Scripture, the Church—all of it. Of course, many feminist theologians welcome such alterations.

But we must understand that both androcentrism and feminism are failures in terms of understanding the Catholic religion. First of all, these are philosophies that demand an allegiance all their own and claim a priority over the faith of the Church. They carry principles that suppress and misinterpret the revelation of God because they stand outside the revelation and propose to sit in judgment of it. It is not the revelation of God which determines the validity of the feminist perspective; rather feminism and women's experience determines the validity of the revelation.

The relation between sexual gender and authority in the Catholic Church cannot be understood from either an androcentric or feminist perspective. This is because neither view of reality confronts the Christian mystery as it actually exists. Redemption is neither male-centered nor female-centered—it is covenantal. Androcentrism and gynocentrism fail to explain the equal dignity of men and women because they do not understand male and female relations in terms of a one-flesh unity that respects the goodness of God's created order.

THE RADICAL FEMINIST VIEW OF CHRIST

According to its website, Circle of Grace Community Church is "an inclusive feminist worshipping community." Located in Tucker, Georgia, its weekly liturgies are presided over by Pastor Connie in which its members "share the Eucharist and words like these are spoken":

> There is nothing you have to do or say or believe to be fed this holy meal. From the beginning of time the Holy One has fed the people. From the fruit of the garden to manna in the desert, to meals that call us to remember the stories of divine activity of liberating people from oppression. If for any reason you do not wish to share this meal, we ask that you still come be a part of the circle, for this meal must never, must never be a test of who is inside and who is outside the circle. Bread for the journey. Drink in the promises of God.

Whatever worship is taking place at the Circle of Grace Community, the above quote illustrates well several principles of feminist thought, in particular the avoidance of any distinctions essential to feminism. Here there is an absence of doctrinal definitions—as everyone can eat the "holy meal" no matter what they "do or say or believe," the emphasis on becoming "part of a circle"—as circles have no points of differentiation, no tests of "who is inside and who is outside." Within that circle no one, of course, has any "higher place" of authority, so as to realize inclusivity and equality.

The feminist horror of distinction forces even the person of Christ to fit into an egalitarian model of authority. Feminist authors have a tendency to degrade not only the divinity of Christ but His special, unique role as Redeemer of the world. The egalitarian model of justice demands that even Christ be more or less just one person among others. Feminism believes it is wrong for a person or a privileged class of persons, like priests, to claim that they possess special powers to mediate God's divine presence. If Jesus is special, it is because He demolished unjust hierarchical structures and ushered in the new age of egalitarian justice. Jesus is a savior in this sense. Hierarchical structures are a later corruption of the original message of Christ.

In the patriarchal ethic of power, men are associated with mediating divinity to the world. The male Catholic priest as symbol of Christ the Savior is the one symbol feminists most associate with the subjection and oppression of women. Because the Catholic priesthood is intrinsically bound to the celebration of the Eucharist, it is against these two symbols in the Church that feminist theology launches its most severe attack. But the feminist challenge to these sacramental symbols of faith really begins with a crisis of faith regarding the person and work of Christ Himself, as He appeared as Savior in the form of a male human being.

Rosemary Radford Ruether is one of the most well known and influential feminist theologians. Here is what she says about the person of Christ:

In traditional Christian theology, Christ is the model for this redeemed humanity that we have lost through sin and recovered through redemption. But Christ as a symbol is problematic for feminist theology. The Christological symbols have been used to enforce male dominance, and even if we go back beyond masculinist Christology to the praxis of the historical Jesus of the synoptic Gospels, it is questionable whether there is a single model of redeemed humanity fully revealed in the past. This does not mean that feminist theology may not be able to affirm the person of Jesus of Nazareth as a positive model of redemptive humanity. But this model must be seen as partial and fragmentary, disclosing from the perspective of one person, circumscribed in time, culture, gender, something of the fullness we seek. We need other clues and models as well, models drawn from women's experience, from many times and cultures.[3]

Feminist theology is struggling to find a symbol of redeemed humanity, but not even Jesus is adequate to the task! Jesus as a model is "partial and fragmentary." Christ is only one person whose effectiveness as a symbol is burdened by his gender, culture, and history. One of the chief problems with feminist theology is its despair of history. History, rather than being the proper medium of God's Word, actually stands as a barrier to that Word. This is an ancient despair that marks man's religious consciousness prior to the Judeo-Christian revelation. A constant religious temptation is man's desire to escape this corrupted corporeal world, corrupted because corporeality is itself corruption, and get back to that pure world of God and spirit. But this is not the way of the Jew or the Christian. We are saved in the world, through the world, precisely because the world is good and God has an intimate relation to it.

---

3. Rosemary Radford Ruether, *Sexism and God-Talk: Toward a Feminist Theology* (Boston: Beacon Press, 1983), 114.

Feminists are looking for some other model of redeemed humanity, but history and corporeality relativize and degrade any model. So feminists are forced to live in a fragmented world where the "fullness of redeemed humanity is only partially disclosed."[4] In feminism, religious symbols are arbitrary and never absolute because they are burdened by time and kept in service only temporarily until human consciousness evolves to the next stage and renders the symbols obsolete.

Radical feminists reject Christ as the sole model of redeemed humanity because his masculinity enforces male dominance. But what they fail to appreciate is that Christ *alone* is not the sign of redemption. Feminism, since it is a monist system of thought, suffers from a Christomonism that leads to a despair of redemption being effectively mediated in history. Feminism fails to see that redemption is not summed up by the male Christ alone who must then, if He is truly Lord, bring everything into one under the dominance of His power like a pagan god would do. Redemption is not mediated by the male Christ alone, but by Christ and the Church. Redemption is mediated through the covenant. The Church gives a creative response to the mission of Christ that is authentically her own. Thus she is a model of redemption in union with her Lord and has responsibility for the covenant that is equal in human and mediatorial freedom, and thus in dignity to His. Christ is model and source of redemption only in union with the Church.

Not only do feminists feel threatened by the maleness of Christ, but even more threatening to them is the notion that redemption comes from the action of a single individual upon whom everyone is now dependent. This destroys egalitarianism. Equality, and especially so called equality in leadership, is achieved by eliminating the necessity of Christ's sacrifice as the single source of the world's salvation. Elisabeth Schüssler Fiorenza, the feminist biblical scholar, finds

---

4. Ibid.

Jesus' death as atonement for sin repugnant. She claims that this is a later interpretation by only some segments of the "Christian movement," but in no sense does the God of Jesus demand atonement. She states explicitly, "The death of Jesus was not a sacrifice and was not demanded by God but brought about by the Romans."[5]

Christ's death is theologically significant only in the sense that He is killed as a result of His message in the same way that other prophets like John the Baptist were violently put to death. But Jesus' death is not salvific. His death is not the will of the Father, nor is it the means whereby sin is atoned for and man reconciled to God by the grace won by His Son.[6]

Christ emptied Himself of all power when He permitted Himself to be nailed to a cross. Yet, ironically, feminists believe that it is precisely Christ's sacrifice that is part of the patriarchal system of power and domination. It is the sacrifice of Christ that constitutes Him a priest, and thus as a priest Christ possesses power no human individual can be said to possess or exercise. In other words, Christ's priesthood means He has something we do not have. Women are especially deprived because Christ only shares His sacrificial priestly authority with certain males of the human race.

One feminist author writes that if men and women are to be equal the priesthood must be disassociated from the sacrifice of Christ and thus from its source of power.

It is to proclaim the end of the priesthood of the temple in favor of the Christian priesthood. In this way we leave power all its position, a firmly human position which no function can any longer assume in the name of God. The God of Jesus is neither the god eager for sacrifices for whom his own son would be the only satisfactory victim, nor the god of the renewal of this expiatory sacrifice, be it merely an

5. Fiorenza, *Memory*, 130.
6. Ibid., 135.

efficacious symbolic action. He is the God who saves man's longing in a work of life. Hence priesthood cannot and must not dig itself in behind an efficacious symbolism in order to defend the prerogatives of a masculine institution of *potestas sacra*.[7]

The egalitarian tendency is at work in this quotation. Power cannot be exercised in God's name, in the name of an entity greater than and separate from man. And if power is a human thing, the sacrifice of Christ must be abolished. It certainly cannot ever be re-presented in an "efficacious symbolism." The priesthood, which feminists abhor as an elitist class, depends on this symbolism. One need not wonder what would become of the Catholic faith if the re-presentation of Christ's sacrifice were absent.

The sacrifice of Christ on the Cross as the source of salvation is rejected in feminist theology because such a sacrifice is a threat to the feminist view of equality. If Christ's person and personal work is salvific, this means that some one possesses a "power," a "quality" that stands outside of the world and Church, over and against the world and Church upon which people are made absolutely dependent. The Catholic priesthood perpetuates the otherness of God and Christ, and this type of distinction between the sacred and profane gives rise to hierarchical systems of domination and dependency—if not oppression. If equality is to be real, Christ must not possess anything that the Christian community does not possess. Notice how Ruether denigrates the importance of the historical person of Christ and his uniqueness as Savior and blurs the distinction between Him and the Church.

---

7. Marie Zimmerman, "Neither Clergy nor Laity: Women in the Church" in *Women Invisible in Church and Theology*, ed. Elisabeth Schüssler Fiorenza and Mary Collins, *Concilium*, 182 (Edinburgh: T & T Clark, Ltd., 1985), 33.

Christ as redemptive person and Word of God, is not to be encapsulated "once-for-all" in the historical Jesus. The Christian community continues Christ's identity. As vine and branches Christic personhood continues in our sisters and brothers. In the language of early Christian prophetism, we can encounter Christ in the form of our sister. Christ, the liberated humanity, is not confined to a static perfection of a person two thousand years ago. Rather, redemptive humanity goes ahead of us, calling us to yet incomplete dimensions of human liberation.[8]

In a certain sense Ruether is right. The Church does "continue Christ's identity." Christians have "put on Christ" through Baptism. In the sacraments Christ shares His redemption with the faithful. However, feminist theology hesitates to make any real distinction between Christ and the Church because distinctions are the seeds of inequality. In the feminist idea of Eucharist there is very little emphasis on Christ as an object of worship. In short, Christianity is no longer the worship of a "person."[9] The community is not turned towards Christ as source of its salvation and praise. Gone too are any effective symbols such as the ministerial priesthood and the consecrated species which are causative of the Church's worship.

The feminists seek to reform the Catholic faith by dissolving its hierarchical clerical structure to make way for the egalitarian community in keeping with what they believe to be Jesus' original vision of redemption. In such a community all Christians are empowered by the Spirit and no one individual or special caste in the Church has exclusive claim to represent the presence and power of God. It needs to be clarified that the most influential feminist theologians do not believe in the Catholic priesthood. If they rally for the ordination of women, its accomplishment is merely a political step towards

8. Ruether, *Sexism*, 138.
9. Ibid., 211.

abolishing clergy altogether. The abolition of the clergy is certainly the goal promoted by feminists' chief theological spokesperson. Ruether's views on this are well worth quoting.

> The liberation of the Church from clericalism also means reclaiming the sacraments as expressions of the redemptive life of the Church that the people are empowered to administer collectively. The community may designate various people at different times to develop and lead liturgical expressions, but this does not mean these persons own or possess a sacramental power that the community does not have. Rather, it means these persons represent and gather into a collective experience the sacramental life process of the people. . . . Reappropriation of the sacraments means that not only the exercise but also the interpretation of the sacraments arises from the community's collective experience of its life in grace. The baptism of each individual involves all members of the community, who midwife each other's rebirth from alienated to authentic life. Penance means forgiving one another. It is not the disciplinary tool of any elite. Eucharist is not an objectified piece of bread or cup of wine that is magically transformed into the body and blood of Christ. Rather, it is the people, the ecclesia, who are being transformed into the body of the new humanity, infused with the blood of new life. The symbols stand in the midst of and represent that community.[10]

In the feminist Church there is no priesthood that acts *in persona Christi*. There is no Sacrament of the Eucharist that has efficacy *ex opere operato* ("from the work worked"), in other words from the objective power of the ritual itself. The entire sacramental economy has been revised. Sacraments are not the actions of Christ. They are

---

10. Ibid., 208–9.

simply the community's actions "arising from the community's collective experience." This is, of course, consistent with feminist theology that begins and ends with women's experience and not the revelation of God. The feminist Church is a dismally flat Church, so much so that even those who lead the "liturgical expressions" are designated by the community in a pristine democracy. Nothing—no person, no symbol—stands over/against the community in relation to the community.

Those who lead liturgies are not representing Christ. They represent the faith community. At this point we have a Church turned in on itself. Its liturgies are exercises in narcissism. The Eucharist is no longer worship of Christ, Lord and Savior, in which He is objectively present as source of that worship. The Eucharist represents the Church. But this Church is not Christ's Body either (a Body that is the complement of and in relation to its Head). Instead, the Eucharist represents the "new humanity."

The horror of distinction permeates all aspects of feminist theology. The quest for unity, dignity, and equality among all human beings, and most especially between men and women, is an ancient quest. Feminist theologians are by no means alone in their desire for unity and equality at the expense of the goodness of God's created order. Feminist theology departs radically from the Catholic faith regarding the relation between history and the validity of the sacramental priesthood. The Catholic Church teaches that her sacraments and doctrinal teaching flow from the covenant instituted by the one sacrifice of Christ Himself. The sacraments and doctrinal tradition are essential to the Church's historical mediation of the one sacrifice. Any development of sacramental worship occurred in history under the inspiration of the Holy Spirit.

THE RADICAL FEMINIST CHURCH

Most non-Christian philosophies consider history to be the enemy of truth. Feminism shares this suspicion of history. Historical circumstances weighted with the corruption of human influence cause truth and justice to be obscured or perhaps not even possible to obtain at all. For the ancient pagan, salvation is achieved by getting out of the world and being joined to the pure other world of spirit from which the world of matter is a Fall.

Feminist theology regards historical circumstances as the enemy of Christ's original pristine message that was supposed to usher in the egalitarian community of justice. This is the opinion of Fiorenza. The Christian religion was corrupted very early when, forced by its surrounding Greco-Roman culture, it moved from charismatic leadership (meaning leadership prompted solely by the Spirit) not based on role differentiation, to hierarchical office. Fiorenza's interpretation of Scripture is controlled by the idea that Christ's mission was to show compassion for the poor and the outcast and put forth anti-authoritarian statements such as "call no one your father" (Mt 23:9), etc. For her these things serve as the models for understanding what the kingdom of God and salvation are all about. Galatians 3:27–28 is the principal Scripture passage that expresses the essence of Jesus' mission. Feminists in the Church have adopted it as a kind of manifesto: "For as many of you as were baptized into Christ have put on Christ. There is neither Jew nor Greek, there is neither slave nor free, there is neither male nor female; for you are all one in Christ Jesus."

Fiorenza argues that the egalitarian vision of the early Christians was a threat to the pagan patriarchal order. Christians accepted slaves and women into the Church. Political classes and the privilege of the elite are abolished in favor of the "new humanity" in which all are equal in Christ. The Christian religion was particularly attractive to the socially denigrated, i.e. slaves and women, because it "promised them liberation from the patriarchal order."[11]

This inclusive vs. exclusive community of equals is, according to Fiorenza, later replaced by hierarchy and office as the Church begins to accommodate itself to the ethics and behavior of the time.

Greco-Roman culture is based on hierarchical relationships with power located in a dominant male authority figure. Fiorenza states that when Paul and Peter instruct wives to be subject to their husbands, children to obey their parents, and slaves to obey their masters in what are known as the "household codes" (Eph 5:22, 6:1–8; 1 Pet 2:13–3:6), they do so as a result of a Greco-Roman patriarchal influence.[12]

Contrary to the paterfamilias, early Church authority is characterized by role interchangeability. According to Fiorenza, in the early Church all Christians, based on their baptism, had equal access to authority, leadership, and power. If she is correct, Christianity must have been corrupt from nearly the very start. The notion that everyone was potentially equally a leader is simply not supported by the New Testament witness. The mere fact that Christ surrounded Himself with twelve handpicked males to constitute the foundation of the Church with Peter as the head demolishes the feminist interpretation that authority was established by Christ according to an egalitarian model.

Fiorenza is in total agreement with Ruether that no one possesses a sacramental power that the community as a whole does not possess. Ruether also characterizes the early Church as a millenarist, egalitarian, spirit-filled community. But a conflict soon developed between the "original; charismatic order" and the emerging institutional order. Ruether portrays the conflict as a struggle for power in which the institutional office of the bishop emerged as victor.

---

11. Fiorenza, *Memory*, 265.
12. Ibid., 263–4.

If this were really the case, how does one account for the silence in the New Testament letters about this conflict? Many other conflicts are reported in detail, especially by St. Paul. If there was a conflict such as Ruether describes with the office of the bishop winning, one would expect to see some evidence of it in the New Testament literature. After all, Ruether contends that the institutional ministry "felt the need" to cut off the charismatic prophesying that was characteristic of a Church in its infancy. Here is how she describes the conflict:

> Those who continue to speak in the name of Christ become heretics (Montanists). Revelation is said to be closed and located in the past in a historical Christ and a past apostolic community. The ongoing power of the Spirit sent by Christ to the community is no longer to "blow where it will" but is institutionalized in the authority of the bishops. They receive the original "deposit of faith" from the apostles and they pass it down unaltered in their official teaching traditions. Both the interpretation of the words of Christ and the power of reconciliation with God is to be wrested from the hands of the charismatics, prophets, and martyrs and placed in the hands of the episcopacy, which takes over the claims of apostolic authority.[13]

According to the feminist view of history the story of the Church is one of a pure original community that almost from its inception fell gradually more and more into a corrupt view of authority and power as it succumbed to the unjust patriarchal culture around it. The sacramental system, male priests, and the authority of bishops are the result of historical corruption. The cure for this corruption is to go back to the beginning and uncover the true vision of Christ.

For women to achieve equality in the Church, the Church's doctrinal history must be revised by feminists to recover the tra-

13. Ruether, *Sexism*, 124.

ditions of early Christian sects that supposedly advocated the
equality of women but which were condemned as heretical by the
"orthodox" Church.

FEMINISM AND GNOSTICISM

This feminist return to the original moment when the Christian faith
was pure is characteristic of feminism's despair of history. We have
already noted the feminist repugnance for distinctions, but feminism also has a problem appreciating matter, and radical feminist
theology seeks salvation outside of this temporal world. It has much
more in common with Gnosticism than with the Judeo-Christian
view of reality.

Gnosticism is an ancient philosophical/religious system of
which there were many forms. It predates the Church by hundreds
of years and was also contemporary with her. Despite its many cults
and sects it is marked by several definite characteristics. Gnosticism
is a radically dualist system which believes things of the spirit, mind,
or soul are utterly incompatible with matter. The world of matter is
evil, including the human body. This corrupted world must be fled,
escaped, overcome, etc., if salvation is to be achieved by the spirit
alone. Indeed, it is matter that keeps the human spirit separated from
God, or keeps persons from realizing their own divinity.

It is this world of matter that causes divisions, that makes things
to be separate and fragmented, such as the division between male
and female. Salvation means being rid of this fragmentation of life,
and having one's spirit joined to the world of the spirit that is not
weighed down by the corruption of matter and knows no division.
Justice is found in the single monist unity of spirit which exists outside of time.

Only a very few, however, will come to possess the knowledge
necessary to achieve this salvation since the knowledge is secret and

conveyed only to a minority. This system is termed "Gnosticism," which comes from the Greek word *gnosis*, meaning "knowledge."

Mary Daly is probably the chief spokesman for a feminist theology that seeks salvation, and only the salvation of women, by having them escape this evil temporal realm. She unabashedly articulates this type of soteriology in her books *Beyond God the Father* and *Gyn/Ecology*. According to Daly, not only is Christianity irretrievably sexist, but the entire world has been corrupted by male influence. Men are responsible for all the world's evils.[14] Men have produced the "Most Unholy Trinity" of rape, genocide, and war. The greatest evil men perpetuate is their quest to dominate and eliminate all that is feminine from the world. Like Dracula, men actually feed on the bodies and minds of women. The He-male lives on women's blood. The patriarchal forces of the male world sap and suck out the life energies of women.[15] For Daly, salvation is salvation from this oppression. But it means, a la the platonic/gnostic route, that the woman must escape this temporal realm.

> Breaking through this male Maze is both exorcism and ecstasy. It is spinning through and beyond the fathers' foreground which is the arena of games. This spinning involves encountering the demons who block the various thresholds as we move through gateway after gateway into the deepest chambers of our homeland, which is the Background of ourselves.[16]

Women accomplish this escape by turning in upon themselves where the woman, retiring into herself, "dis-covers" her "Be-ing." It is within the self alone, isolated and apart from the world, apart from

---

14. Mary Daly, *Beyond God the Father: Toward a Philosophy of Women's Liberation* (Boston: Beacon Press, 1973), 114–122.

15. Ibid., 172–3.

16. Mary Daly, *Gyn/Ecology: The Metaethics of Radical Feminism* (Boston: Beacon Press, 1978), 2.

men, that salvation is achieved. The woman possesses herself and creates herself and in so doing creates the "Otherworld."[17]

Ruether mildly criticizes Daly's notion of redemption as "primarily spiritual."[18] However, her own version of man's redemption is also utterly incompatible with the Christian insistence on the good of man and woman, the individual self, and creation. Her book *Sexism and God-Talk: Toward a Feminist Theology* is important if for no other reason than she is one of the first thinkers to provide a comprehensive, systematic feminist theology that goes way beyond simply the issue of women's ordination. When I read the book I thought, "I know where this theology is going. I know where it will ultimately end." But I also thought: "Ruether, who still wants to be regarded as a thinker within a Christian framework, will go to the edge of radical feminist thought but pull back from that edge. She won't go over the cliff." As I kept reading, however, I found that she did in fact go over the cliff and plummet. I thought that if feminist theology wants to be consistent it will have to argue that no real distinction exists between God and matter—and thus leap off the cliff of Christianity with such an assertion. Since for Ruether, as well as for Daly, injustice is rooted in differentiation, Ruether indeed eliminates even a proper distinction between spirit and matter. According to her, even God is not simply a spiritual being. The "God/ess" is both spirit and matter:

> The God/ess who is primal Matrix, the ground of being-new being, is neither stifling immanence nor rootless transcendence. Spirit and matter are not dichotomized but are the inside and the outside of the same thing. When we proceed to the inward depths of consciousness or probe beneath the surface of visible things to the electromagnetic field that is the ground of atomic and molecular structure, the visible disappears. Matter itself dissolves into energy. Energy, or-

---

17. Ibid., 340.
18. Ruether, *Sexism*, 231.

ganized in patterns and relationships, is the basis for what we experience as visible things. It becomes impossible anymore to dichotomize material and spiritual energy.[19]

Stated simply, spirit and consciousness are only different forms of matter. There is no transcendent God who exists as Other than the world. All reality—spirit, matter, God—is the same entity. Therefore, not only can it be said that men and women do not differ from each other in any significant way, but there is no significant difference between God and nature. Ruether is trying to achieve unity in a world seemingly torn and atomized and thus filled with injustice. However, salvation for her is not a matter of getting out of the world as it is for Daly. In a sense, Ruether goes to the other extreme but for essentially the same reasons.

In *Sexism and God-Talk*, Ruether asks whether immortality serves feminism. Rather, she should ask whether feminism serves immortality. Because Ruether regards differentiation as the enemy of unity, her theology inevitably preaches the annihilation of the individual. The self must be erased. This is salvation. She explains that with death, personal consciousness comes to an end.

Consciousness ceases and the organism gradually disintegrates. This consciousness is the interiority of that life process that holds the organism together. There is no reason to think of the two as separable, in the sense that one can exist without the other.

What then has happened to "me"? *In effect, our existence ceases as individuated ego/organism and dissolves back into the cosmic matrix of matter/energy, from which new centers of individuation arise. It is this matrix, rather than our individuated centers of being, that is "everlasting," that subsists underneath the coming to be and passing away of individuated beings and*

19. Ibid., 85–6.

even planetary worlds. Acceptance of death, then, is the acceptance of the finitude of our individuated centers of being, but also our identification with the larger matrix as our total self that contains us all.[20] (Emphasis added)

Salvation is annihilation. How utterly dismal! Gone is the immortality of the soul. Gone is the resurrection of the body. Gone, it would seem, is any personal love between God and me. Feminist theology solves the ancient problem of the One and the Many by wiping out the Many. Justice and harmony are achieved by a collapse of the Many into the cold, unloving, depersonalized One, or, as Ruether calls it, the "cosmic matrix of matter/energy." None of this is compatible with the Christian faith.

While the Christian is alive, the One is the Christian community, and when he/she dies it is the earth that swallows up everything erasing all distinctions. Ruether tries to soften this picture by stating that the individuated self is not lost, only changed. What is the change? We become food for new beings to arise from our bones.[21] This is still a rather bleak prospect. Ruether's doctrine essentially rediscovers a primitive notion of reincarnation. This is a Lion King theology in which we are all just a part of the never-ending "circle of life." The individual person is lost. A person's transcendence means simply being food for other selves. The individual person is utterly insignificant, an idea completely contrary to the Christian religion that affirms the reality and goodness of each person made in the image of God.

Daly may be among the most radical feminist theologians, but in a real sense hers is the quintessential statement of where feminist theology leads. It does not matter that her idea of salvation for women is a spiritual salvation of the Mind while Ruether's seems to emphasize the eternal life and goodness of the Earth. Both views

20. Ibid., 257.
21. Ibid., 258.

deny the goodness of human sexuality. The individual self insofar as it is a sexual, concrete, physical entity is not important and in the end is destroyed. Ruether tries to escape Daly's completely spiritualized salvation but only succeeds in providing a clever camouflage for what is still fundamentally a pessimistic and un-Christian view of human beings and their relation to God and to the world. The ancient Gnostics sought to escape the body (that is, the individual self) so that the person's divinity could be realized or the soul joined to the one cosmic spirit free of all temporal corruption. Ruether's thought differs from this only in the sense that instead of escaping matter, matter becomes the One in which the self is dissipated.

The feminist horror of distinction must deny the goodness of the created order. In His creative act God named something else—something other than Himself—as good. The Christian religion teaches that it is possible for something to be good and not be God Himself. Unless we want to be pagans, this distinction between God and His creation must be affirmed. Furthermore, because God's creation rests on the beauty of a covenantal differentiation, the primary symbols of this covenant are male and female persons, who though distinct are yet one flesh. Salvation is not a monist annihilation of the self, thus it does not annihilate sexual difference. This difference is from the Beginning and possesses a transcendent religious meaning. The way male and female sexuality serve the redemptive order of grace is the basis for male and female authority in the Catholic Church.

3
THE MEANING OF MALE
AUTHORITY IN THE CHURCH

The Quiet Man is a 1952 film directed by John Ford and stars John Wayne and Maureen O'Hara. Wayne plays ex-boxer Sean Thornton, who retired from the sport after accidentally killing a man in the ring. He seeks quiet and solace for his tortured soul by returning to Innisfree, an idyllic Irish village where he was born. With plans to settle there permanently, Thornton purchases a lovely whitewashed cottage. He soon courts the gorgeous and high-strung Mary Kate Danaher, but her older brother Will Danaher is opposed to their marriage and will not give his consent, much less the expected dowry. The villagers trick Will into believing that if he allows the wedding, the local wealthy widow will consent to marry him. After Sean and Mary Kate exchange vows, Will learns that the wealthy widow isn't interested in him after all, and he thus stubbornly refuses to give Kate her dowry. As a consequence, Kate refuses to consummate the marriage with Sean and insists that he demand the dowry from her brother. Sean, however, couldn't care less about the dowry and won't go after it. Kate accuses him of cowardice, not realizing that Wayne's character is haunted by his having killed a man in a boxing bout and now has moral and psychological aversion to violent confrontations. Film critic Rob Nixon states:

O'Hara's Mary Kate Danaher is no demure Irish lass. She's tough, outspoken, aggressive, stands up to her brother, wallops men and bridles at the term "spinster." She's hell bent on maintaining her identity and independence even after marriage by insisting her husband fight for the money and household goods that are rightfully hers but denied by her stubborn, bullying sibling. "In characteristic American fashion, he feels his masculinity and ability to provide for her impugned, until she finally makes him understand that it is not the money but what it stands for," remarked critic Molly Haskell. "The dowry and furniture are her identity, her independence."[1]

Another critic, Brandon French, notes that the movie is lauded for its depiction of a liberated woman who is clearly her husband's equal. Towards the end of the film, when Sean and Mary Kate are planting a garden, a sign that they have peacefully settled into their domestic future, she whispers in his ear and together they joyfully race back to the cottage. It is clear that, on her initiative, the couple will at last become one flesh. Earlier in the film she rejects her husband's attempts to control her by "tearing from his hands the stick another woman has given him to beat her and throwing it away. His delighted acquiescence to this act (and to her suggestive whisper at the end) is indicative of the sexual equality Ford depicts in this relationship. This enlightened treatment of sexuality promotes, as few American films have, the superiority of a mature and liberated love relationship," French writes.[2]

The conflict between them, however, is overcome when Sean finally takes action against Mary Kate's brother. When Mary Kate takes steps to leave him, Sean roughly drags Mary Kate to the broth-

---

1. Turner Classic Movies, Rob Nixon, http://www.tcm.com/tcmdb/title/24069/The-Quiet- Man/articles.html

2. Ibid.

er's house and flings her at Will's feet demanding that he take her back or give her the dowry. Will begrudgingly flings the money at his feet. Mary Kate takes the money and escorting Sean to a stove throws it into the fire, proving that the money itself was not the issue but only what it represented, her own liberation and freedom from the mastery of her brother. Before the couple consummate their bond, Sean and Will thrash their differences out in a grand fistfight. Will, bested by the boxer, endures his humiliation with manly valor and thus wins the heart of the local widow after all.

This charming classic film demonstrates an important aspect of masculine authority. In a sense Sean had to prove he was a man; he had to prove himself a worthy husband by fighting for what rightfully belonged to his wife. It was only when he was ready to stand up for her, defend her, and advocate for her that the marriage really could take place.

The ultimate fulfillment of authority,—and dare I say—masculine authority, is the manner in which Christ exercises headship to the Church. He is responsible for her. He is responsible for her both in the sense that He is the cause of her existence and that He cares for her as the vehicle of His presence in the world. Thus authority is the possession of the one who gives life. In this chapter we will take a closer look at the meaning of Christ's headship and thus discover the meaning of male ecclesial authority itself.

Feminists believe that authority, if it is to be freed from a despotic kind of rule, must be freed from a hierarchical structure. So, for them, church leaders will be designated "from below" by the community, even those leaders who preside over the liturgy. These new church leaders will not derive their power through an ordination rite and, of course, Holy Orders as a sacrament would no longer exist. As Ruether said, those who lead "liturgical expressions" do not possess a sacramental power that the community does not have. In a sense, then everyone in the church is a ministerial priest.

The feminist proposal looks democratic, even, and fair. But practically speaking this system of leadership would create elitism within the Church never experienced in the Sacrament of Holy Orders. Who will be the new leaders? They will be the ones most educated, most intelligent, perhaps even the wealthiest, and the most ambitious. Church leadership that is not rooted in the sacramental system soon descends into sheer politics. A priest should not essentially be honored or respected because of his personal charisma, intelligence, and talents. He is to be respected because he is a sacramental icon of Christ and this transcends all politics.

CHRIST'S HEADSHIP

The redemption of man is made possible by the authority of God. The authority of God is present through His Son who is now forever in union with His Church. The reality of Christ's authority is spoken liturgically in the Eucharist, where the believer is put into the most intimate contact with the power of salvation. It must always be kept in mind that Christ is in union with His Church and that it is through this bond, and not apart from it, that salvation is effected in the world. The reality of this bond is liturgically spoken by men and women who express the covenant of salvation. Authority in the Catholic Church is the power to effect supernatural life. This supernatural life is not given apart from the covenant of Christ and the Church, whose unity is inherently nuptial.

The headship of Christ is frequently misunderstood to mean that He has the power of domination over the Church and over all of creation. Everything is subjected to Him. This idea of headship is closer to the notion of power via strength. In other words, Christ is Head because He is God and can suppress and place in order what is less than Himself. Headship as the strength to dominate means that Christ exercises His authority extrinsically to the Church and creation. The power to dominate means that He is not really in a loving unity with the Church. Christ rules by the force of His strength as God which renders Him the Church's Lord and Master.

But the headship of Christ, and thus His authority, really is something other than simple domination by strength. To be head means that one is a source of life or the beginning of something. This is the sense of the word as it is found in St. Paul's Letter to the Ephesians. One of the most important New Testament passages on Christ's headship is Ephesians 1:19–23:

> And what is the immeasurable greatness of his power in us who believe, according to the working of his great might which he accomplished in Christ when he raised him from the dead and made him sit at his right hand in the heavenly places, far above all rule and authority and power and dominion, and above every name that is named, not only in this age but also in that which is to come; and he has put all things under his feet and has made him the head over all things for the Church, which is his body, the fullness of him who fills all in all.

Christ dominates the cosmological powers, but His relationship to the Church is much different. Christ subjects all rule and authority to His rule. The above passage shows Him sitting "far above" these other powers. The Father has put all things under Christ's feet. We really have the idea that the powers are put down by force. But this is not the relation of the Head of the Church to His Body. The Church is distinctly separated from the passage about domination. Christ is not said to be "far above" her, spatially separated from her. Instead, the Church is one with Christ. She is His Body.

St. Paul does not say that Christ is Head of all things including the Church. Rather, in the original Greek the passage states that Christ is "head over all things to (or for) the Church." Christ is exalted precisely because He has subdued all powers opposed to the kingdom. Now Christ can be Head of the Church in His glory and triumph, which is to say, Christ can be her Head because He has subjected all other powers for her. The Church as Christ's Bride has an exalted Head and she is in a privileged position in relation to Him.

Scripture studies show that the word *head* has two meanings. One sense is "overlord," but the other sense is "source" or "beginning."[3] In other words, Christ is the principle of the Church's existence. St. Paul would have in mind the Old Testament sense of the word *head*, which means "first" or the "beginning" of something. For example, Genesis 2:16 speaks of the river in Eden having four heads—the start of four other rivers. In the Septuagint, the ancient Greek translation of the Old Testament, the words *head* and *beginning* are often interchangeable. *Ruler* was sometimes designated by the word for *head* in Greek (Jude 11:11; 2 Sam 22:44) or by the word for *beginning* (Ex 6:25; Mic 3:1).[4]

Colossians 1:18 says of Christ: "He is the head of the body, the Church; he is the beginning, the first-born from the dead, that in everything he might be pre-eminent." Headship here is not simply "ruler." Rather, Christ is the principle of creation and redemption.

HEADSHIP AND THE SACRIFICE OF CHRIST

Christ is the Head of the Church because He has given Himself up for her. The Church has life because Christ died. Ephesians 2:13–16 explicitly teaches that Christ is the source of the Church's being because he died for her:

---

3. S. Bedale, "The Meaning of in the Pauline Epistles," *Journal of Theological Studies*, 5–6 (1954–1955), 212–13; Stephen F. Miletic, "'One Flesh': Eph 5.22–24, 5.31 Marriage and the New Creation," *Analecta Biblica*, 115 (Roma: Editrice Pontificio Istituto Biblico, 1988), 74.

4. Bedale, "The Meaning," 212–13.

> But now in Christ Jesus you who once were far off have
> been brought near in the blood of Christ. For he is our
> peace, who has made us both one, and has broken down the
> dividing wall of hostility, by abolishing in his flesh the law
> of commandments and ordinances, that he might create in
> himself one new man in place of the two, so making peace,
> and might reconcile us both to God in one body through
> the cross, thereby bringing the hostility to an end.

Ephesians 1:22–23 declared that Christ is the Head of the Church which is His Body. The above passage from the same epistle tells us that this Body is formed from Jews and Gentiles. Christ who is the Head of this Body is so as its source. He is the cause of a new creation, a new man, specifically through His death on the Cross.

Christ's sacrifice is the cause, source, and origin of the Body which in Ephesians 5 is called His Bride. Husbands are the heads of their wives, and they are told that their headship must be patterned after Christ's. The pattern is one of sacrifice. And it is specifically Christ's sacrifice associated with His headship that brings the Church to life.

> For the husband is the head of the wife as Christ is the
> head of the Church, his body, and is himself its Savior. . . .
> Husbands, love your wives, as Christ loved the Church and
> gave himself up for her, that he might sanctify her, having
> cleansed her by the washing of water with the word, that he
> might present the Church to himself in splendor, without
> spot or wrinkle or any such thing. (Eph 5:23–27)

Christ and the Church, the Head and the Body relation, exist according to the "one flesh" of the first couple. In one of the most remarkable New Testament passages St. Paul quotes the Book of Genesis:

"For this reason a man shall leave his father and mother and be joined to his wife, and the two shall become one flesh." This is a great mystery, and I mean in reference to Christ and the Church. (Eph 5:31–32)

Because headship is linked with sacrifice, this has revolutionary implications for the meaning of authority and the purpose of submission. St. Pope John Paul II has called Ephesians 5 a Gospel "innovation." Christian authority is a radical departure from all that is of this world. Authority is not a matter of lording it over others as Christ Himself taught (Mt 20:25–27). It has to do with power put to the service of life. John Paul II teaches that the Gospel "innovation" of Ephesians 5 is that there now exists mutual subjection between spouses:

> *"Husbands, love your wives,"* love them because of that special and unique bond whereby in marriage a man and a woman become "one flesh" (Gen 2:24; Eph 5:31). . . .
>
> The author of the Letter to the Ephesians sees no contradiction between an exhortation formulated in this way and the words: "Wives, be subject to your husbands, as to the Lord. For the husband is the head of the wife" (5:22–23). The author knows that this way of speaking, so profoundly rooted in the customs and religious tradition of the time, is to be understood and carried out in a new way: as a *"mutual subjection out of reverence for Christ"* (cf. *Eph* 5:21).[5]

This mutual subjection is possible because the headship of Christ is connected to his sacrifice:

> The husband is called the "head" of the wife *as* Christ is the head of the Church; he is so in order to give "himself up for

---

5. Pope John Paul II, Apostolic Letter On the Dignity and Vocation of Women *Mulieris Dignitatem* (August 15, 1988), no. 24.

her" (Eph 5:25), and giving himself up for her means giving up even his own life. However, whereas in the relationship between Christ and the Church the subjection is only on the part of the Church, in the relationship between husband and wife the "subjection" is not one-sided but mutual.

In relation to the "old" this is evidently something "new": it is an innovation of the Gospel.[6]

John Paul II states that between Christ and the Church subjection is on the part of the Church only. But it is very important that we not miss the fact that Christ already subjected Himself to her. He gave up His very life so that she may be exalted in holiness. Christ's authority is life-giving and He has given Himself for the Church in the most radical subjection of all.

The subject of submission is an extremely touchy one. It is so touchy that the American bishops have allowed Colossians 3:18 to be edited from the Mass readings on the Feast of the Holy Family. The verse teaches: "You who are wives be submissive to your husbands." This edited version of the Sunday reading went into effect January 10, 1993. Undoubtedly, like inclusive language, the alternative reading was permitted so as not to offend women and promote misunderstanding, and as a concession to feminist thinking. But it shows that bishops, priests, and many lay people simply do not know how to deal with the subject of submission—particularly feminine submission—and so the topic is simply avoided altogether or treated as something so much a part of an ancient world view that it is just not relevant for us today. The redemptive value of submission is understood by first appreciating that submission exists even within the Godhead. The Son is subject to the Father. First of all, Christ is sent by God (Jn 5:36). Secondly, in His messianic mission Christ does what He sees the Father doing: "The Son can do nothing of his own

------

6. Ibid.

accord, but only what he sees the Father doing" (Jn 5:19). In the spirit of true submission Christ even says: "For I have come down from heaven, not to do my own will, but the will of him who sent me" (Jn 6:38). The submission of Christ to the Father's will is so complete that it leads Christ to His death on the Cross. This is the lesson of Gethsemane; "Father not my will, but yours, be done" (Lk 22:42).

Certain passages in the New Testament, like the one in Colossians, seem only to exhort women to exercise submission. But if the self-offering of Christ the Head is taken seriously, and if husbands are to be heads as Christ is Head, then they too practice a real kind of submission within the one-flesh unity.

What purpose does marital submission serve? Firstly, it is never to be confused with subjugation in the sense of an inferior party being subservient to a superior one. Submission, whether on the part of the husband or wife, exists for the sake of their marital unity. In other words, one obeys for the objective good of the marriage so that marriage, as it is designed by God, may flourish. And so, even the husband may have to listen to his wife if she is calling him to act for the good of their bond.

CHRIST THE CORNERSTONE

Headship and source are explicitly identified in Ephesians 2:19–22 and 4:15–16, as well as Colossians 2:19. Ephesians 2:19–22 is a statement about the Church composed of Jews and Gentiles:

> You are fellow citizens with the saints and members of the household of God, built upon the foundation of the apostles and prophets, Christ Jesus himself being the cornerstone, in whom the whole structure is joined together and grows into a holy temple in the Lord; in whom you also are built into it for a dwelling place of God in the Spirit.

The Church (or building) is not its own cause. It is "built upon the foundation of apostles and prophets" with Christ alone as the central stone of the structure. Christ is the source of the structure's unity and order. It is through Him that the whole structure is fitted together. It is in the Lord that the building grows into a holy temple. *Grows* is the original Greek word translated as "takes shape" in the above quotation. The builder of the edifice is Jesus Christ.

The Church "being built" reminds us of the beginning of creation and thus places this Christ/Church unity into a marital context. Ephesians 2:19–22 uses a form of the Greek verb "to build" twice in the passage, i.e. "being fitted together" and "being built into this temple." The Septuagint uses the verb in Genesis 2:22. Here, after casting Adam into a deep sleep, God "built up into a woman the rib that He had taken from the man" (NAB). To build the first woman and to build the Church draws a correlation between them: they are the first and the second Eve.

As the first Adam is the source of the first Eve, so Christ is the source of the Church's life. We see the marital dimension of this also in that Christ is not separate from the structure of whom He is the cause. J. Armitage Robinson points out: "He is part of the Body which He brings into being, for He is its Head: He is part of the house which He founds, for He is its cornerstone."[7]

Ephesians 4:15–16 also teaches that the Head is the source of the Body's growth and unity:

> Rather, speaking the truth in love, we are to grow up in every way into him who is the head, into Christ, from whom the whole body, joined and knit together by every joint with which it is supplied, when each part is working properly, makes bodily growth and upbuilds itself in love.

---

7. J. Armitage Robinson, *St. Paul's Letter to the Ephesians* (London: James Clarke & Co. Ltd, 1922), 68.

A parallel passage in Colossians 2:19 states:

. . . and not holding fast to the Head, from whom the whole body, nourished and knit together through its joints and ligaments, grows with a growth that is from God.

These passages clearly show that Christ is not the Head because He dominates the Church by a rule of power. He is Head because He is the Church's vivifying principle.

CHRIST THE NEW ADAM

In Ephesians, Christ is Head because by His sacrifice He is the source of the Body. The Head and the Body exist according to a marital one-flesh unity (Eph 5:21). In St. Paul's Letter to the Romans, Christ is the Head (or source) of the Church (the new creation) because He is the New Adam.

Therefore as sin came into the world through one man and death through sin, and so death spread to all men because all men sinned—sin indeed was in the world before the law was given, but sin is not counted where there is no law. Yet death reigned from Adam to Moses, even over those whose sins were not like the transgression of Adam, who was a type of the one who was to come.

But the free gift is not like the trespass. For if many died through one man's trespass, much more have the grace of God and the free gift in the grace of that one man Jesus Christ abounded for many. . . .

Then as one man's trespass led to condemnation for all men, so one man's act of righteousness leads to acquittal and life for all men. For as by one man's disobedience many were made sinners, so by one man's obedience many will be made righteous. (Rom 5:12–19)

Adam and Christ are the origins of two races of men. The first Adam is the source of the mankind of sin and death. The second Adam is the source of the mankind of righteousness and life. Both Adam and Christ are an original ancestor.[8] Christ functions as a first patriarch of a new creation in contrast to the old head who acted in disobedience. The actions of the two heads have radically different results for their offspring.

Romans calls Adam the "type of one who was to come." Adam, in other words, is a foreshadowing of Christ, the New Adam. Adam is a type of Christ in that, like Christ, he is the beginning (or head) of a people. Furthermore, Adam was created as the image God had for humanity. Adam ruined this image by sin. Christ restored it. The true meaning of the first Adam is definitively revealed in the second. There is a correlation between creation and redemption that is willed by God.

The great Protestant theologian Karl Barth has noted that both Adam and Christ are alike, as both are one source for "the many." But if the correlation between creation and redemption is a true one, Adam is not simply a type of Christ because his action (in this case sin) determined the destiny of all men. Adam is the cause of sin for all because he stands at the beginning as the primordial source of man. Christ is Head because He definitively and gloriously fulfills the role and place of Adam as the new beginning, the source of the "one new man" (Eph 2:15) which is the Church.[9]

The Letter to the Romans teaches that the New Adam brings the Church to life by His sacrifice on the Cross. St. Paul contrasts the old Adam's single offense, an act of disobedience, to the New Adam's

---

8. Robin Scroggs, *The Last Adam: A Study in Pauline Anthropology* (Philadelphia: Fortress Press, 1966), 106–7.

9. Karl Barth, *Christ and Adam* (New York: Octagon Books, 1956), 58–9.

single righteous act of obedience. The headship of the New Adam cannot be disassociated from the offering up of His life. As Romans 5:6–10 states:

> While we were yet helpless, at the right time Christ died for the ungodly. . . . Since, therefore, we are now justified by his blood, much more shall we be saved by him from the wrath of God. For if while we were enemies we were reconciled to God by the death of his Son, much more, now that we are reconciled, shall we be saved by his life.

Christ's headship exists in that He is the New Adam who has given up His life for the New Eve, His Body, the Church. Colossians 1:15–20 repeats many of the themes found in Romans regarding the New Adam. In these verses from Colossians, Christ is the beginning of a new people as He is "the first-born of all creation." Christ, who is source of all creation in that all in heaven and earth was created "in him" (1:16), is also called Head of "the body, the Church" (1:18). Colossians goes on to describe this headship specifically as Christ being a beginning and a source of life when it says: "he is the beginning, the first-born from the dead" (1:18). Finally, the headship of Christ is linked to His power of reconciliation by the offering of His blood, "the blood of his cross" (1:20).

The headship of Christ and thus His authority is bound to the giving up of His life. The New Adam gives life to the Church in His sacrifice. St. Augustine powerfully described the love of this New Adam in all of its nuptial beauty.

> But where did [Christ] sleep? On the Cross. When He slept on the Cross, He bore a sign, yea, He fulfilled what had been signified in Adam: for when Adam was asleep, a rib was drawn from him, and Eve was created; so also while the Lord slept on the Cross, His side was transfixed with a

spear, and the Sacraments poured forth, whence the Church was born. For the Church the Lord's Bride was created from His side, as Eve was created from the side of Adam. But as she was made from His side no otherwise than while sleeping, so the Church was created from His side no otherwise while dying.[10]

MALE AUTHORITY IN THE CHURCH

The Church teaches that males, and more specifically, ordained males, are a sacramental sign of Christ in the world. *Inter Insigniores* (Declaration on the Admission of Women to the Ministerial Priesthood) provides a number of arguments in support of the male priesthood. Its first argument is from what is called the Church's "constant tradition." Christ called only men to the priesthood and the Apostles remained faithful to the will of the Lord in this matter. Moreover, the Church believes Christ's attitude in calling only men to the priesthood has a permanent value and is not the result of the cultural constraints of the time. After all, Christ frequently broke with the prejudices of His time regarding the status of women.

The document goes on to explain that the priest acts *in persona Christi*, "taking the role of Christ, to the point of being his very image." Since the priest is a sign, the sign must be perceptible, and therefore the one who acts *in persona Christi* must bear a "natural resemblance" to Christ who, after all, "was and remains a man."

One of this document's formally theological arguments is from the Christ/Church relationship. *Inter Insigniores* teaches that the relation between Christ and the Church is marital. From Old Testament times the covenant took on "the privileged form of a nuptial mystery." This nuptial mystery comes to completion in the unity between

---

10. St. Augustine, "Ennarations on the Book of Psalms," 127,4, *The Nicene and Post-Nicene Fathers*, Vol. 8, ed. Philip Schaff (Grand Rapids, MI, 1956), 607 (PL 37. 1672, Ps 126, 7).

Christ and His Church. Christ is the Bridegroom of His Church who
is His Bride.

> That is why we can never ignore the fact that Christ is a
> man. And therefore, unless one is to disregard the impor-
> tance of this symbolism for the economy of Revelation, it
> must be admitted that, in actions which demand the char-
> acter of ordination and in which Christ himself, the author
> of the Covenant, the Bridegroom, the Head of the Church,
> is represented, exercising his ministry of salvation—which
> is in the highest degree the case of the Eucharist—his role
> (this is the original sense of the word *persona*) must be taken
> by a man. This does not stem from any personal superiority
> of the latter in the order of values, but only from a difference
> of fact on the level of functions and service.[11]

It is very clear that Christ's sexuality, His male gender, is significant to the economy of salvation. Catholicism takes sexuality—
and the sexuality of Christ—seriously. A person's sexuality cannot
be dismissed as if it had nothing to do with salvation. Notice that
Inter Insigniores more than once emphasizes that Christ is a man.
Not only was He a male human being while on the earth but, as we
already discussed, even in His glorified state He "remains a man."
This means that a person's sexuality has a transcendent, eternal dimension. Even St. Augustine, for all his Neoplatonism, taught that
human beings rise from the dead, male or female. Salvation does not
mean that only the soul is saved. We are not Gnostics or Platonists,
but Christians who believe the body is good and is an inherent part
of what it means to be human.

To understand Christ's authority in relation to the Church requires understanding that Christ gives life specifically as a male.
Christ does not give life to the Church apart from the significance of

---

11. *Inter Insigniores*, sec. 5.

His male gender. His life giving function is performed from "within" this gender. Therefore, masculinity is the proper symbol of how Christ, the Son of God, gives life.

The Church's being rests on the fact that Christ Himself historically established her worship. Christ Himself guarantees that the worship the Church offers is efficaciously pleasing to the Father. The Father will accept this worship because the Eucharist is the one sacrifice of Christ offered by Christ's own authority.

The great French theologian Cardinal Henri de Lubac profoundly and succinctly articulated the essence of priestly power. He states some of the principles by which priestly power is inherently connected to male sexuality. Regarding the sacramental priestly character he writes:

> Those who are invested with it, whatever the human circumstances of their appointing, participate in the Church's mission to engender and maintain the divine life in us, and this by a delegation from God Himself. Christ, the true and only Priest, has chosen them as the instruments through which He is to act upon us, and to this end passed on to them what He received from His Father.[12]

Priestly authority is bound to male sexuality because of the relation between the headship of Christ and His engendering of the Church. This is the way that Christ exists as source. Furthermore, the divine life that is transmitted to the Church through the priesthood is received by her. The Church's life is bestowed upon her from the outside. The Church is not her own cause. The male is related to priestly action because the meaning of masculinity does not rest in itself. Masculinity receives its symbolic value by being a transparency for what is transcendent as opposed to what is immanent. The

---

12. Henri de Lubac, *Splendour of the Church* (Glen Rock, NJ: Paulist Press, 1956), 84.

male human being is a sign for God because, like God, the male, even if he is the most caring and loving husband, nevertheless remains detached and separated from what he creates through his sexual acts. Because he is removed from creation in a way that women are not, men image what is other than nature. Through the Sacrament of Holy Orders a priest is more than only a sign of Christ. Holy Orders also makes real in the world a truth about the fatherhood of God. The male priesthood speaks a truth about the authority of God, about how God relates to the world.

By entrusting His authority to males, Christ preserves a truth about His love in relation to His creation. His sacrifice is uniquely His own offered for the Church. The particularity of His sacrifice has its historical and eternal expression in the marital order of the New Covenant. In marriage, nothing can substitute for the unique gift a husband makes to his wife and the wife to her husband. Similarly, Sean in *The Quiet Man* had to do something for Mary Kate, rather than Mary Kate simply doing it for herself. The gift of self is embodied in a personal word of the man as man and the woman as woman. Out of this unique self-donation the unity of their one flesh is formed. The male sexuality of the priesthood speaks the uniqueness of Christ's gift of self. Christ makes a complete personal self-donation that is the cause of a unique covenantal response on the part of the Church. A bisexual priesthood renders the unique self-donation of Christ unintelligible. The economy of Christian worship would be dissolved. The feminist quest for a female priesthood is based in the mistaken idea that all words are basically the same, in this case: the word of the human body. Feminism believes that symbols as such are meaningless, that revelation has no language with which to speak except what is contrived from one culture to the next.

Feminists tend to view the male and female body as virtually irrelevant. The person is what matters to them and what the person is able "to do," despite their sexual gender. It is as if, true to Gnosticism, the real person somehow exists apart from his gender. For the feminist, gender should not matter when considering whether someone is "qualified for the job." But when "the job" entails imaging the marital/covenantal love and authority of God in the world, the bodily significance of male and female sexuality cannot be dispensed with. The human body as man or woman—indeed, the entire person as man or woman—serves as the communicator of God's covenantal love.

CHRIST REVEALS THE FATHER'S LOVE

Christ's authority to the Church is entirely bound to His sacrifice as Bridegroom. It is this authority that Christ entrusted to His Apostles. The following passages show clearly the inherent connection between the Lord's leadership and the giving up of His life.

> I am the good shepherd. The good shepherd lays down his life for the sheep. He who is a hireling and not a shepherd, whose own the sheep are not, sees the wolf coming and leaves the sheep and flees; and the wolf snatches them and scatters them. . . .
>
> I am the good shepherd; I know my own and my own know me, as the Father knows me and I know the Father; and I lay down my life for the sheep. And I have other sheep, that are not of this fold; I must bring them also, and they will heed my voice. So there shall be one flock, one shepherd. For this reason the Father loves me, because I lay down my life, that I may take it again. (Jn 10: 11–17)

Christ's authority is associated with His ability to give life. As John 10:10 states: "I came that they may have life, and have it abundantly." Regarding Christ's authority, however, the voice of the Good Shepherd is not His alone. Christ's authority and priesthood is en-

tirely bound to His mission of revealing the Father. The voice of the
Good Shepherd is the voice of the Father spoken through the Son,
and the authority of both Father and Son is linked with their ability
to give life. The Gospel of John teaches that the Christ's work is the
work of the Father (5:17). This work is the result of a most intimate
relation between the Father and the Son (5:19–20). The essence of
the work of Father and Son is to give life:

> For as the Father raises the dead and gives them life, so also
> the Son gives life to whom he will. (5:21). . . .
>
> For as the Father has life in himself, so he has granted
> the Son also to have life in himself, and has given him au-
> thority to execute judgment, because he is the Son of man.
> (5:26–27)

An intimacy and dependency exists between the Father and the
Son. The incarnate Son of God exists as a type of sacrament of the
Father's will and action. Christ states: "The words that I say to you
I do not speak on my own authority; but the Father who dwells in
me does his works" (Jn 14:10). This and many similar passages dem-
onstrate that Christ's mission reveals the Father.[13] Christ is the icon
of the Father's life-giving love. However, is it really necessary for the
Church to insist that the salvation of the world is bound to the masculine symbol of God as Father? Is Father merely a name for God or
does the word Father reveal a truth about God that feminine symbolism is incapable of communicating?

THE FATHERHOOD OF GOD

God is Father because He is the cause of His people while remaining separate in nature from His people. Yahweh is the totally Other.
Creation is from God and stands in relation to God. The great insight

---

13. See page 20 of chapter one for a list of Johannine passages.

of the ancient Hebrew faith is that something that is not God could itself be good as the first chapter of Genesis repeatedly testifies. An I-Thou relationship exists between God and what He has made. Creation is good and can actually glorify God and give Him praise. Creation, while outside of God, is not therefore evil as the ancient pagan philosophies and religions believed. The psalmist declares: "All your works shall give thanks to you, O Lord, and all your saints shall bless you! They shall speak of the glory of your kingdom, and tell of your power" (Ps 145:10–11). God is Father also in that He alone is the cause of the Hebrew nation. The Hebrew people exist because they are in a covenant with God that He initiated. The work of salvation in Christ began under the Old Covenant when God called the Hebrew people to be His own. God is the cause of their liberation from slavery in Egypt so that He could make a covenant with them at Mt. Sinai. This covenant was the beginning of the fulfillment of the promise God made to Abraham. This promise had its first seed bestowed in the birth of Isaac.

The fatherhood of God is perhaps nowhere more vividly displayed than in the fact that He opens the barren womb of Sarah, enabling her to be a mother—indeed, the mother of a nation. God does this beyond all human power. Through Abraham and Sarah God engenders for Himself a people. The near sacrifice of Isaac, the son of promise, illustrates the power of God as Father. Genesis 22 relates the story of how Abraham is told by God to kill his only son, upon whom every hope of the Hebrew nation rests. When Abraham is ready to plunge the knife into the child, God intervenes again to give life. Isaac and the promise of a Hebrew nation are actually re-engendered by God. God reveals Himself as Father over and over again in the Old Testament. Life is received by creation, by Israel, by barren women where there is no life.

It is the Holy One of Israel who opens or closes the womb. Even the first child, Cain, caused his mother Eve to acknowledge the procreative power, not of Adam, but of God: "I have produced a child with the help of the Lord" (Gen 4:1). . . . When Sarah or Hannah or (in Luke's Gospel) Elizabeth conceived, it is a triumph of the woman and the Lord. One is almost given the impression that the earthly father is an instrument and bemused observer of it all.

This theme of God's liberating paternity reaches its apex with Jesus, who was literally "the Son of God. . . ." One could almost say that it takes not two to make a baby, but three: a man, a woman and the Holy Spirit.[14]

The mother of seven sons in 2 Maccabees 7:22–23 who watched the torture of her children proclaimed:

> I do not know how you came into being in my womb. It was not I who gave you life and breath, nor I who set in order the elements within each of you. Therefore the Creator of the world, who shaped the beginning of man and devised the origin of all things, will in his mercy give life and breath back to you again, since you now forget yourselves for the sake of his laws.

This mother proclaims the key to understanding God's paternity: He "devised the origin of all things." But while God is Father, because He is the principle of all that exists, these Old Testament women experience their power to conceive in relation to God. God does not take over their place. He does not substitute for them in their power to give life. Rather He causes them to be mothers. God also reveals

---

14. Juli Loesch, "God the Father," *The National Catholic Register* (Feb. 26, 1984), 5.

Himself as Father to His people in the restoration of Israel following the Babylonian exile.

> I will make them walk by brooks of water, in a straight path in which they shall not stumble; for I am a father to Israel, and Ephraim is my first-born.
> "Hear the word of the Lord, O nations, and declare it in the islands afar off; say, 'He who scattered Israel will gather him, and will keep him as a shepherd keeps his flock.'" (Jer 31:9–10)

The power of gathering and scattering is God's as He alone is the source of life and unity for His people. Fathering and shepherding are linked in the above passage from Jeremiah. In the new dispensation, Christ fulfills the role of the shepherd who is the *arche* of His people, and in this role He reveals the Father. The sacrifice that the Good Shepherd offers gathers together a people:

> I lay down my life for the sheep. And I have other sheep, that are not of this fold; I must bring them also, and they will heed my voice. So there shall be one flock, one shepherd. (Jn 10:15–16)

This passage is about bringing together the Jews and the Gentiles into one Body. This parallels Ephesians 2:13–26 where this gathering together is accomplished through the Cross of Christ. John's Gospel also specifically states that Christ's death is the source of a new people: "Unless a grain of wheat falls into the earth and dies, it remains alone; but if it dies, it bears much fruit" (Jn 12:24). The phrase "it remains alone" means that the man who tries to guard his life will remain alone and singular, but when the Son of Man dies He will become the origin of many, the Head of a new people. In John 12:32 Jesus again explains the meaning of His death: "And I, when I am lifted up from the earth, will draw all men to myself."

God's fatherhood causes the Jews to be a people. Christ, as the Son who reveals the Father, is the origin of the new people of God. The prophet Ezekiel speaks of God as a shepherd who draws together the scattered sheep because the shepherds who were in charge of the sheep oppressed and exploited them. But the true shepherd will rescue them and give them the choicest places to graze (Ezek 34:11–14). God's authority is based on the benevolent care He has for His sheep. Indeed, His authority is contrasted with the misuse of authority by Israel's leaders, who lorded their authority over the flock "with force and harshness" (Ezek 34:4). Now we see clearly the true meaning of authority. God's fatherhood and His shepherding are not despotism. His authority is not mere quantitative power. Authority is measured by the power to give life and the care that one has for others.

The shepherding role of Christ is the expression of the Father's love. The work of Christ is the work of the Father who brings a people into being. Christ's authority, His headship, is entirely bound to what it means for Him to reveal the Father. What He reveals is the supreme creative love of the Father which is definitively expressed in Christ's sacrifice and is the source of the Church. The masculinity of Christ cannot be dissociated from the type of love He reveals. As in the Trinity, the mission of Christ to reveal the Father's love is relationally ordered. The Father as principle of the Son is unique in His giving. The Father's place is not interchangeable. If the Father's love is unique, the symbol of its expression to us in the world must also be unique. The marital order of the world and of redemption manifests the unique love of the Father in the headship of the Son, who is Bridegroom to a feminine Church that has its origin in Him. The Church has her own unique gift to make to the Father, a sacrifice of praise, which is not interchangeable with the sacrifice of the Bridegroom.

THE AUTHORITY OF MALE PRIESTS

The authority of Christ, Shepherd and Head who reveals the love of the Father, is the authority entrusted to the Apostles whom He personally commissioned. Christ taught the Apostles that "He who receives you receives me, and he who receives me receives him who sent me" (Mt 10:40). In the Gospel of John, this commissioning formula is repeated: "Truly, truly, I say to you, he who receives any one whom I send receives me; and he who receives me receives him who sent me" (Jn 13:20). Later on in the same Gospel Jesus gave the Apostles the authority to forgive sin, stating: "As the Father has sent me, even so I send you" (Jn 20:21).

These passages clearly indicate that Christ's mission of redemption is the result of having been sent by the Father. His authority is rooted in being sent. This fact means that Christ is outside of the Church, in relation to her, and cannot be confused with her. The Mystical Body of Christ is not the result of Christ absorbing the Body into Himself. Rather it is the consequence of a free unity that causes Christ and the Church to become "one body." In the pattern of Christ's authority, the Apostles are likewise sent by Him. They become icons of His salvific authority. As His representatives, the Apostles have a sacramental function. They sacramentally represent Christ and because Christ was sent by the Father, the Apostles derivatively are signs to the Church of the Father's love.

Christ the Good Shepherd shows that authority and sacrifice are joined. It is precisely the authority of the Good Shepherd that Christ entrusts to the Apostles and their successors. The salvific authority of Christ, which is passed on to the Apostles, is the authority to offer the unique sacrifice of Christ which is the source of the Church. The Apostles' authority is Eucharistic. The Eucharist is the celebration of the marriage covenant between God and His people.

Christ spoke of His authority as that of a Good Shepherd who gives life. The sacrifice of the shepherd is the sacrifice of the Bridegroom who espoused the Church in the shedding of His blood. Therefore, Christ's priestly authority and the authority He passed on to the Apostles are fundamentally male in character. It is a male authority because, rooted in the covenant between God and His people, it reveals the fatherhood of God and Christ as Bridegroom to the Church.

The espousal of God and man begins with the Old Covenant as the prophet Hosea proclaimed: "I [God] will espouse you for ever; I will espouse you in righteousness and in justice, in steadfast love, and in mercy. I will espouse you in faithfulness; and you shall know the Lord" (Hos 2:19–20).

This nuptial mystery comes to its completion with the death of Christ. Marriage is the essence of the covenant. Within this maritally structured covenant the mystery of Christ's sacrifice is revealed. Christ's authority to the Church is bound to His sacrifice. This authority is entrusted to St. Peter and the other Apostles. In the Gospel of John, Christ asks Peter three times, "Do you love me?" and Peter is commissioned to lead and tend the flock of Christ. This leadership takes the form of feeding the sheep (Jn 21:13–17). The scene in John's Gospel is filled with great Eucharistic significance: "Jesus came and took the bread and gave it to them, and so with the fish" (Jn 21:13). The authority given to Peter is to feed the sheep of Christ, to give the Church the food of eternal life. Christ's authority is bound to His sacrifice, and the sacrifice is the giving up of His own body which is the cause of the Church. The Apostles are commissioned by Christ to offer His sacrifice, whereby in this one true act of worship Christ and His people are made one-flesh. Hierarchical priestly authority was established by Christ at the Last Supper.

> At the Last Supper, on the night when He was betrayed, our Savior instituted the eucharistic sacrifice of His Body and Blood. He did this in order to perpetuate the sacrifice of the

Cross throughout the centuries until He should come again, and so to entrust to His beloved spouse, the Church, a memorial of His death and resurrection: a sacrament of love, a sign of unity, a bond of charity, a paschal banquet in which Christ is eaten, the mind is filled with grace, and a pledge of future glory is given to us.[15]

The Eucharist founded by Christ is nothing less than a true sacramental representation of His sacrifice on the Cross by which the New Covenant between Himself and the Church is established. Christ willed "to perpetuate the sacrifice of the cross throughout the ages." The authority of the priesthood rests on this will of Christ. The Eucharistic sacrifice and male priestly authority were instituted on the same night.[16] A priest's authority rests in a sacramental power to effect the sacrifice of Christ which is entirely linked to His headship to the Church. Pope Paul VI's encyclical *Mysterium Fidei* affirms that the Eucharistic sacrifice and the institution of the priesthood are inherently connected.

> For, as the Evangelists narrate, at the Last Supper "he took bread, and blessed and broke it, and gave it to them, saying, This is My Body, given for you; do this for a commemoration of me. And so with the cup, when supper was ended, This cup, he said, is the new testament, in my Blood which is to be shed for you." And by bidding the Apostles do this in memory of Him, He made clear that He wanted it to be forever repeated.[17]

---

15. Second Vatican Council, The Constitution on the Sacred Liturgy *Sacrosanctum Concilium* (December 4, 1963), no. 47.

16. Council of Trent, Sess. 22, Ch. 1.

17. Pope Paul VI, Encyclical Letter On the Holy Eucharist *Mysterium Fidei* (September 3, 1965), no. 28

The Council of Trent also teaches that the Apostles were made priests at the same time Christ instituted the Eucharist "commanding them and their successors in the priesthood to make the same offering."[18]

The essence of Christ's headship is that He is the source of the Church's life and being by His death on the Cross. Priestly male authority stands in the place of Christ the Head. The power they have to perpetuate His sacrifice is given to them by Christ. It is Christ's power. A priest's authority is of a particular kind. It comes from a sacramental manifestation of Christ as priest, meaning Christ as Head—meaning Christ as cause of the Church by His sacrifice. Priests are life-givers to the Body of Christ because they sacramentally extend the salvific work of Christ.

The priest's participation in the headship of Christ exists for the sake of worship. It exists so that the Eucharist may be a true celebration of Christ's union with the Church. This union is caused by the Head having given Himself up for her. Priests sacramentally effect the personal and unique love of Christ the Bridegroom. Cardinal de Lubac, relying on St. Leo the Great, expressed the marital nature of redemption made present in the Eucharist.

> "The participation of the Body and Blood of Christ effects nothing short of this, that we pass over unto that which we receive." The head and members make one single body; the Bridegroom and the Bride are "one flesh." There are not two Christ's, one personal and the other "mystical." And there is certainly no confusion of Head with members; Christians are not the "physical" (or eucharistic) body of Christ, and the Bride is not the Bridegroom. All the distinctions are there, but they do not add up to discontinuity; the Church is not just a body, but the body of Christ; man must not

---

18. Council of Trent, Sess. 22, Ch. 1.

separate what God has united—therefore "let him not separate the Church from the Lord."[19]

The marital nature of the Eucharist preserves what is unique in
male and female responsibility for the faith. This responsibility of the
sexes was established "in the beginning." Adam is the source of Eve
and Eve confers on him his identity and purpose and is mother of
all the living. The worship of the Church is constituted by a marital
freedom and responsibility.

> This worship, centered on the eucharistic sacrifice, the *Chris-
> tus totus*, has therefore the structured, the qualified freedom,
> of the marital relation inherent in the New Covenant, in
> which the sacrifice offered *in persona Christi* by the priest is
> not competitive with the Church's sacrifice of praise, but is
> creative of it, and qualitatively distinct from it. Any ecclesi-
> ology which cannot accept this "model" of freedom in the
> Church has substituted an abstraction for the reality.[20]

By the authority Christ has conferred on priests, He Himself
"builds up, sanctifies and rules his Body."[21] Redemption is possible
because of Christ's own righteous act. The act is His own! Therefore,
only Christ could commission the Apostles to "do this in memory
of me." The Apostles have received a real authority. How could the
Apostles, or anyone, dare to repeat Christ's action unless they had
been given the authority to do so from Christ Himself? Because the
Eucharistic sacrifice is Christ's own action, it can be offered only *in
persona Christi*—only by one authorized to stand in His person, for
in no other persona could the Eucharistic sacrifice be made.[22]

19. De Lubac, *Splendour*, 91–2.

20. Emmett Cardinal Carter, *Do This in Memory of Me: Pastoral Letter on the
Sacrament of the Priesthood*, Dec. 8, 1983 (Archdiocese of Toronto, CAN), 26.

21. Second Vatican Council, *Decree on the Ministry and Life of Priests
Presbyterorum Ordinis* (December 7, 1965), no. 2.

22. Pierre Beniot, "The Accounts of the Eucharist and What They Imply," in *The*

When a priest stands *in persona Christi* the goodness of creation is affirmed. A priest sacramentally stands in the place of the New Adam who embraces the New Eve. Here masculinity and femininity know their beauty, their value, and their truth because they know their differentiated responsibility in effecting the New Covenant. The society of the *Christus totus* is a one-flesh union and the Eucharistic sacrifice is its expression.

> The Eucharistic sacrifice is denied when its covenantal and marital structure is denied. Christ is present in the Mass by the sacrificial "work" through which He is the Head of the bridal Church. This self-offering evokes and creates the Church, whose actuality is her own sacrifice, the distinct self-offering of the Body. In this sacrificial presence of the *Christus totus,* the unique sacrifice on the Cross is One Flesh with the Church's sacrifice of praise, in a union which depends upon their qualitative, marital, irreducibility.[23]

The validity of the Eucharist is attacked if a woman were to attempt to stand *in persona Christi*. This is so not only because Christ is a man, but also because man and woman are the symbols of the New Covenant. Through the difference and unity of the sexes the covenant itself is expressed. The idea of a female priesthood attacks the economy of salvation. Thus any Mass offered by a woman is inherently invalid because the marital truth of the covenant is not spoken. In fact, a female priesthood mixes up the language of worship and makes what ought to be worship something unintelligible. The idea of a female priesthood expresses something other than the covenant. The issue here is not simply that a female priest would take on an authority she does not possess, but rather a female priesthood would

---

Eucharist in the New Testament (Baltimore and Dublin: Helicon Press, 1965), 82.

23. Carter "Do This is Memory of me," 23-24.

rob women of their own special, particular, and unique authority without which the covenant could not exist.

It is to this authority that we must now specifically turn our attention.

4
THE AUTHORITY OF MARY

I cannot now remember whether she was naked or clothed. If she were naked, then it must have been the almost visible penumbra of her courtesy and joy which produces in my memory the illusion of a great and shining train that followed her across the happy grass. If she were clothed, then the illusion of nakedness is doubtless due to the clarity with which her inmost spirit shone through the clothes. For clothes in that country are not a disguise: the spiritual body lives along each thread and turns them into living organs. A robe or a crown is there as much one of the wearer's features as a lip or an eye.

But I have forgotten. And only partly do I remember the unbearable beauty of her face.

"Is it? . . . is it?" I whispered to my guide.

"Not at all," said he. "It's someone ye'll never have heard of. Her name on earth was Sarah Smith and she lived at Golders Green."

"She seems to be . . . well, a person of particular importance?"

"Aye. She is one of the great ones. Ye have heard that fame in this country and fame on Earth are two quite different things."

"And who are these gigantic people . . . look! They're like emeralds . . . who are dancing and throwing flowers before here?"

"Haven't ye read your Milton? A thousand liveried angels lackey her."

"And who are all these young men and women on each side?"

"They are her sons and daughters."[1]

We start this chapter with a lengthy quote from C.S. Lewis' *The Great Divorce*. It illustrates one of the most important aspects of authority—though if we base our idea of authority on notions of quantitative strength and power, publicly enshrined, then indeed Sarah Smith could not be regarded as "a person of particular importance." Indeed, while Sarah lived she appeared to be of no real consequence, living a small, apparently ordinary obscure life in someplace called "Golders Green." However, according to spiritual truths, the ones that really matter, Sarah is "one of the great ones."

She is described by Lewis as having many children—those that she birthed into life by her charity. By her own charity she caused all those who came into touch with her to love others more. She is described as having power to "awaken all the dead things of the universe into life."

Sarah Smith exercised a true motherhood and exercised authority according to this role. Indeed, due to this woman's splendor, the main character of the Lewis story at first mistakes Sarah Smith for Mary, the Mother of God. But Sarah Smith is not really like Mary simply because many show her reverence. Sarah is like Mary because they both, in a most unassuming way, lead people to the fullness of life.

---

1. C.S. Lewis, *The Great Divorce* (Harper: San Francisco, 1946), 118–9.

If we don't locate the essence of authority in this principle, then it is easy to conclude that Mary had little to no authority. And because authority is often primarily associated with official quantitative power over others, feminist theology does not have much use for Mary. She is either ignored altogether or perhaps rehabilitated as a symbol for liberation theology. In feminist theology, Mary, simply by being a woman, belongs to an oppressed class and thus is a voice for all the oppressed when in her Magnificat she announces the overthrow of unjust systems, as God will "depose the mighty from their thrones and raise the lowly to high places." Mary loses respect among feminists because she is seen as a passive figure, following and not leading, who is ultimately defined according to her procreative powers. Mary has been honored throughout the ages because she is a mother, but motherhood is not held in high esteem these days. Mary's motherhood ties her to the hidden and domestic realm where there is little power and status.

Authority, however, is not simply the exercise of power. Authority is the possession of rights that a creator (or author) exercises so that his or her created work may be maintained and brought to its fulfillment. St. Augustine once stated, "Two parents have generated us for death, two parents have generated us for life."[2] The parents of death are Adam and Eve. We are saved by a New Covenant that repairs, or one might even say, fulfills what was in the beginning. This New Covenant is created by the union and cooperation between the New Adam and the New Eve: Christ and Mary.

Christ is the Head of a new humanity because He is the New Adam whose death is the source of the Church. This is His authority because this is how Jesus is the source of life and redemption. But women also possess authority, as they are the source of life in relation to Him in the completion of the New Covenant. The authority of women is based on what women have been specifically entrusted

---

2. St. Augustine, *Sermo* 22.10 (CCL 41.300).

with, according to the meaning of their gender, for the world's salvation. It was God's expressed will that His divine plan of salvation would not be accomplished without the contribution of Mary, Mother of God.

MARY: SOURCE OF THE INCARNATION

St. Paul declares that interdependency exists between the sexes:

> Nevertheless, in the Lord woman is not independent of man nor man of woman; for as woman was made from man, so man is now born of woman. And all things are from God. 1 Cor 11:11–12

"Man is now born of woman." This is true even of the Son of God. Christ is dependent on the life-giving power of Mary. She made God physically present in human history so that salvation could be accomplished. Christ is from Mary because of her yes, because of her *fiat mihi*. "Let it be [done] to me," declared Mary to the angel. Mary's yes is the beginning not only of her motherhood, but also of the new creation. Redemption is begun with the yes of Mary. The Marian era of grace and mercy was often contrasted by the Fathers of the Church with the era of sin and death that Eve caused by her misuse of power. For the early Fathers, Mary is the source of life, the font of the New Covenant. St. Justin Martyr wrote:

> We know that [Christ] before all creatures, proceeded from the Father by His will and power . . . and by means of the Virgin became man, that by what way the disobedience arising from the serpent had its beginning, by that way also it might have an undoing.[3]

---

3. St. Justin Martyr, *Dialogue With Trypho*, 100, trans. R.P.C. Hanson, World Christian Books, vol. 49 (New York: Associated Press, 1964), 60–1 (PG 6. 710).

Because Christ came "by means of the Virgin" the disobedience of the first woman is undone. Tertullian similarly states:

God recovered His image and likeness, which the devil had seized, by a rival operation. For into Eve, as yet a virgin, had crept the word which was the framer of death. Equally into a virgin was to be introduced the Word of God which was the builder up of that life; that what by one sex had gone into perdition, by the same sex might be brought back to salvation. Eve had believed the serpent; Mary believed Gabriel; the fault which the one committed by believing, the other by believing blotted out.[4]

Women hold the key to death and life. Tertullian seems to think it is entirely appropriate that if death came by a woman, this death should be overcome by a woman. Womankind is not dismissed because in the beginning she brought death. Salvation is not brought by men having to suppress women and keep them in subjugation according to the pessimism of the ancient pagan worldview. Rather, women are fully engaged, free moral agents, able to fulfill their God-given responsibilities for the faith. Tertullian appreciates quite clearly the redemptive power of the female sex.

St. Irenaeus provides one of the most famous passages on the salvific life-giving role of Mary.

But Eve was disobedient. . . . As she, having indeed Adam for a husband but as yet being a virgin . . . becoming disobedient became the cause of death both for herself and for the whole human race, so also Mary, having the predestined man, yet being a Virgin, being obedient, became both to herself and to the whole human race the cause of salvation. .

---

4. Tertullian, *On the Flesh of Christ*, 17, *Ante-Nicene Fathers*, Vol. 3 (Grand Rapids, MI: Wm. B. Eerdmans, 1963), 536 (CSEL 69–70.233).

. . For, whereas the Lord, when born, was the first-begotten of the dead, and received into His bosom the primitive fathers, He regenerated them unto the Life of God. He Himself becoming the beginning of the living, since Adam became the beginning of the dying. . . . And so the knot of Eve's disobedience received its unloosing through the obedience of Mary; for what Eve, a virgin, bound by incredulity, that Mary, a virgin, unloosed by faith.[5]

And, though the one had disobeyed God, yet the other was drawn to obey God; that of the virgin Eve the Virgin Mary might become the advocate. And, as by a virgin the human race had been bound by death, by a virgin it is saved, the balance being preserved, a virgin's disobedience by a virgin's obedience.[6]

Both Christ and Mary are origins of life. Irenaeus states that Christ is "the beginning of the living," but this is only possible through the Virgin's obedience. The saint does go so far as to say that the human race is saved by this Virgin's obedience.

Sts. Cyril of Jerusalem, Ephrem Syrus, and Epiphanius all likewise proclaim that Mary is the cause of new life in God.[7] Mary as source of life in contrast to Eve is proclaimed by St. Jerome in almost the form of a slogan: "Death by Eve, life by Mary."[8]

Mary is not a passive instrument of God. Rather, she is instrumental. She is instrumental in the drama of salvation specifically according to her feminine life-giving powers. Eve was disobedient. Mary is obedient. This means that in their freedom Eve and Mary are real moral agents: they effect death or life for others by their

5. St. Irenaeus, *Against Heresies*, 3, 22, 4, The Ante-Nicene Fathers, Vol. 1 (Grand Rapids, MI: Wm. B. Eerdmans, 1987), 455 (PG 7, 1.958–9).

6. Ibid., 5, 19, 1.547 (PG 7, 2.1175).

7. St. Cyril of Jerusalem, *Catechesis* 12, 15 (PG 33.742); St. Ephrem Syrus, Opp. Syr. ii; St. Epiphanius, Haer. 78, 18 (PG 42.730).

8. St. Jerome, *Letter 22 to Eustochiam* (CSEL 54.173).

personal choices. It is through the authority of Mary's obedience that God became man. The entire economy of salvation is bound up with this fact. In the beginning Eve is taken from the first Adam. In the new beginning the New Adam is taken from the New Eve. By this, St. Paul's teaching is affirmed: "For as woman was made from man, so man is now born of woman. And all things are from God" (1 Cor 11:12).

Mary is God's true partner in redemption and is so precisely through her femininity. God re-created the world through a woman. In the beginning God's word "Let it be done" brought life into being. His divine "fiat" brought forth creation out of nothing. At the Annunciation, Mary becomes the source of the new creation. Now the "Let it be done" is not God's but man's. More specifically it is woman's. Because the Incarnation is the beginning of a new humanity, Mary is the New Eve, mother of all the living, in relation to Christ the New Adam.

MARY AND THE MISSION OF CHRIST

The motherhood of Mary is a redemptive responsibility. She was entrusted with bringing Christ into the world, but her maternity also means that she brings Christ's priesthood to its supreme fulfillment. The mother of Christ helps lead her Son to the Cross. The ministerial priesthood is under the rule of women's responsibility for the faith, as the sacramental order itself is realized through the Marian maternal principle.

Mary is an actual agent of salvation. She is not just a puppet for God who simply makes use of her female biology so that Christ may be present in history. Mary's motherhood means that she actually helps her Son accomplish His redemptive work. When Mary opened her womb to Christ, she gave birth to Him on the Cross.

The maternal authority of Mary is clearly revealed at the wedding at Cana. Here Mary instigates the mission of her Son and leads Him to the Passion.

> On the third day there was a marriage at Cana in Galilee, and the mother of Jesus was there; Jesus also was invited to the marriage, with his disciples. When the wine failed, the mother of Jesus said to him, "They have no wine." And Jesus said to her, "O woman, what have you to do with me? My hour has not yet come." His mother said to the servants, "Do whatever he tells you." (Jn 2:1–5)

This incident is remarkable for a number of reasons. First, Mary takes the initiative in the situation. Jesus says the lack of wine is her concern, but she obviously thinks it is His concern too and expects that he will do something about it. But, of course, the wedding at Cana is not about simply the replenishment of an alcoholic beverage. Jesus' words, "My hour has not yet come," are the key to the meaning of this passage. In the Gospel of John "the hour" refers to Christ's crucifixion and His entrance into glory. Christ's words at Cana, "My hour has not yet come," connect His first miracle to His Passion. The performance of the miracle of changing water into wine will usher in "the hour" which is precisely the reason Christ was conceived and born "of woman." The wedding at Cana shows that Mary is not only the mother of Jesus, she is the mother of His mission. She is the principal human agent in the initiation of Christ to His public ministry. Mary officiates at Cana. Her officiation is directed at aiding her Son in the accomplishment of His work of redemption.

The quality and quantity of the wine produced by Christ demonstrates the messianic import of His first miracle. Mary knew the importance of Christ's first public act.[9] She serves as the catalyst of

---

9. Andre Feuillet, *Jesus and His Mother* (Still River, MA: St. Bede's Publications, 1984), 14.

Christ's salvific activity. Because she leads Christ to His Passion she therefore also leads Him towards His glory. She is not the cause of this glory in the sense that she gave Christ the power to perform the miracle. Christ is God and the power is His. But she acts as the origin of the miracle in the sense of being the facilitator of it, in the same way that Mary exercises authority in the Incarnation. As Mary brought Christ into the world, here she causes Christ's glory to be manifested to the world. Thus she is the origin of the disciples' faith which comes as a result of the Cana miracle (Jn 2:11).

MARY, THE NEW EVE

Christ executed His first miracle because someone requested it. But this someone is not just anyone—it is His mother. It is precisely because Mary is Christ's mother, the source of His presence in the world, that she has the authority to request a miracle that would lead her Son to His Passion. Mary possesses this authority because it is tied to her maternal role in the economy of salvation. As the Mother of God she has been entrusted with aiding Christ in His salvific work. She can send Christ to the Cross because she is the source of His priesthood and thus she has a maternal right to nourish its fulfillment. Indeed, Mary has not only the right, but the responsibility to do so.

When Mary leads Christ to the Cross, she undoes the knot of Eve's disobedience. Eve led Adam away from what it meant for him to be a man and to be the head. Eve brought Adam under the power of her own whim. She misused her feminine power which, as St. John Chrysostom in *Homily IX* stated, led Adam astray from the will of God.[10] The New Eve uses her authority to lead the New Adam, not to do her will, but to accomplish the will of the Father who sent Him.

---

10. St. John Chrysostom, Homily IX, trans. Philip Schaff. "Homilies on Timothy," Nicene and Post Nicene Fathers, Vol. 13, ed. Philip Schaff, (Grand Rapids, MI., Wm. B. Eerdmans), 1962, 435 (PG 62.544).

This is a key element of feminine authority. Feminine authority is meant to lead men to fulfill what it means for them to be masculine and to fulfill the specific tasks and responsibilities with which they are entrusted in the order of creation and redemption. At Cana, Christ subjects Himself to Mary in the accomplishment of His Father's business. Or perhaps we should say that Christ, through the mediation of Mary's maternal authority, discerned and then subjected Himself to the will of the Father. She is the New Eve, the true and effective helpmate of the New Adam.

As the New Eve, Mary is the co-redemptrix. Her role as such is revealed by Christ at Cana when He addresses His mother by the word "woman." This woman of Cana is the woman of Calvary, where Mary accomplished by her maternal authority the covenantal role of the New Eve, whose work, united to the sacrifice of her Son, serves as the origin of mankind's regeneration.

Mary fulfills the promise of the Protogospel. The Protogospel is a verse found in Genesis, chapter three. God confronts the first couple with their sin of disobedience and then turns to the serpent with these words: "I will put enmity between you and the woman, and between your seed and her seed; he shall bruise your head, and you shall bruise his heel" (Gen 3:15).

The passage describes a serious struggle involving the woman, her offspring, and the evil one. The triumph will ultimately be won by the woman's child. St. Justin Martyr identifies the offspring as Christ, who came through the New Eve, whose life-giving obedience he contrasts with the death-giving disobedience of the old Eve.[11]

Eve, not Adam, is at the center of the struggle whereby the world's redemption is won. Yes, Eve was seduced by Satan. Nevertheless, she is most directly involved in undoing the Fall made possible through her because of her life-giving maternal position. Because the

---

11. Justin Martyr, *Dialogue*, 100.

offspring is Christ, Mary is at the center of the redemptive struggle as she fulfills the prophecy of the Protogospel.

The essence of woman is to have authority over the divine gift of life. Because of this, Mary is the source of the New Covenant. The Protogospel tells us that this is the meaning of woman. Woman as "mother of all living" was indispensable to the beginning of creation, so too she is indispensable as the source of the new beginning. John Paul II states this clearly in his apostolic letter *Mulieris Dignitatem*:

> It is significant that the foretelling of the Redeemer contained in these words refers to "the woman." She is assigned the first place in the Protoevangelium as the progenitrix of him who will be the redeemer of man. . . . *Mary is the witness to the new "beginning" and the "new creation"* . . . since she herself, as the first of the redeemed in salvation history, is a "new creation": she is "full of grace." It is difficult to grasp why the words of the Protoevangelium place such strong emphasis on the "woman," if it is not admitted *that in her the new and definitive Covenant of God with humanity has its beginning, the Covenant in the redeeming blood of Christ.* The covenant begins with a woman, the "woman" of the Annunciation of Nazareth.[12]

With the sin of Adam and Eve death came into the world, yet the Fall of Man did not obliterate the fact that woman is still the center of life. The Savior will come from a woman. The Fall could not obliterate her life-giving powers. Indeed, the maternity of Eve constitutes the vital factor in salvation history. From the beginning the woman is identified with her power: she is "mother of all the living" (Gen 3:20).

In 1983 then Cardinal Joseph Ratzinger noted that even after the Fall woman preserves the mystery of life, the power that is opposed to death. Even though Eve brought death, she is nonetheless the

---

12. *Mulieris Dignitatem*, no. 11.

keeper of the seal of life.[13] St. Paul teaches that the turning point in all history is bound to a woman. "But when the time had fully come, God sent forth his Son, born of woman" (Gal 4:4). The feminine authority of the first woman is definitively fulfilled by the Virgin Mary from whom comes the long awaited Messiah. Eve's words of triumph literally apply to Mary. She can say, "I have gotten a man with the help of the Lord" (Gen 4:1).

MARY AND THE CROSS OF CHRIST

The woman of the Protogospel is the woman who will stand at the foot of the Cross on Golgotha and be a true "mother of all living" through the sacrificial offering she makes as the second Eve. The suffering of the woman is an essential part of the work of salvation: "In pain you shall bring forth children" (Gen 3:16). These words apply not only to Eve but also to the New Eve who became the Mother of the Church and of all Christians.

At Cana, Mary is entrusted with the task of ushering her Son to His hour. But the hour is also hers. The pain of Genesis 3:16 that belongs to the woman is scripturally linked to the pain of the Cross. In the farewell discourse of John's gospel Jesus states:

> When a woman is in labor, she has pain, because her hour has come; but when she is delivered of the child, she no longer remembers the anguish, for joy that a child is born into the world. (Jn 16:21)

Salvation's drama is linked to the work of the woman. The woman who instigates Christ's first miracle is the same woman present at the hour of His death. Unfortunately, many bibles translate Christ's words to His mother as "O woman, what have you to do with me?

---

13. Joseph Cardinal Ratzinger, *Daughter Zion* (San Francisco: Ignatius Press, 1983), 17.

My hour has not yet come" (Jn 2:4–5). Such a translation seems to indicate that Jesus places a separation between her seemingly minor concern and His salvific mission. However, the original Greek text literally reads, "What is this to me and to you, woman? My hour has not yet come." Here we see that Jesus, rather than treating Mary as an outsider or someone removed from His hour, actually includes her in it. The hour is not just the hour of the Son. It is theirs. Mary is a partner with Christ in His work of redemption.

The feminine, life-giving power permeates salvation history, bringing it about from the very Beginning. When Christ describes His death in terms of a woman engaged in the painful labor of childbirth, the Protogospel is placed at the center of His Passion. Here on Calvary the woman gives birth to the offspring that will crush the head of Satan. Thus the hour of Cana is the woman's hour as well as Christ's. Mary's "fiat" has brought herself and her Son to the Cross. Both of them have accepted the meaning of the Incarnation. At the Cross Mary's maternity is ultimately fulfilled. There she becomes the mother of all those reborn through the blood of the New Adam.

According to Genesis 3:15, the adversary of the offspring, the evil one, is also the enemy of the woman. Therefore the mother of the offspring is not only present at the Cross but she actually contributes to the victory over the evil one. For this reason Mary is established for all eternity as "mother of all the living." On Calvary the personages of the messianic drama meet each other for the final action. At Calvary Mary is again addressed by Christ as "Woman." Her womanhood is entirely connected to what it means for her to be the universal mother of the disciples.

> But standing by the cross of Jesus were his mother, and his mother's sister, Mary the wife of Clopas, and Mary Magdalene. When Jesus saw his mother, and the disciple whom he loved standing near, he said to his mother, "Woman, be-

hold, your son!" Then he said to the disciple, "Behold, your mother!" And from that hour the disciple took her to his own home." (Jn 19:25–27)

At the Cross Mary's universal motherhood is fulfilled. She is not only the mother of Christ; she is the mother of the faithful whom John, the beloved disciple, represents. Christ exercises His headship supremely from the Cross because it is from there that the Lord becomes the source of a New People. The New Eve stands in direct relation to the headship of Christ, whom as the Protogospel indicates and the New Testament witness affirms, is the covenantal partner in the order of redemption. Because Christ is from her, the Body of Christ, the Church, is derivatively from her. Furthermore, the Bride of Christ, the Church, is made in the Marian image as the Church is the essence of feminine response to the creative action of God. Pope Pius X states:

> Wherefore in the same holy bosom of his most chaste Mother Christ took to Himself flesh, and united to Himself the spiritual body formed by those who were to believe in Him. Hence Mary, carrying the Savior within her, may be said to have also carried all those whose life was contained in the Savior. Therefore all we who are united to Christ, and as the Apostle says are members of His body, of his flesh, and of his bones, have issued from the womb of Mary like a body united to its head.[14]

Because Mary is the mother of Christ, the Head, when she conceived Him she conceived the faithful. Thus she is the mother of the whole Body. This is why her maternity, declared by Christ from the Cross, is not simply a motherhood in the moral sense (as in the case of adoption), or merely symbolism. Mary's motherhood to the

14. Pope Pius X, Encyclical Letter On the Jubilee of the Immaculate Conception *Ad diem illum laetissimum* (February 2, 1904), no. 10.

disciples is a real motherhood and thus a real authority. The Fathers of the Church call Mary the New Eve because by her obedience she is the Mother of the Redeemer and thus the woman through whom the human race is reborn.

THE COMPASSION OF MARY

The Woman is the covenantal partner of Christ. Christ, the priest and the victim, offers the one sacrifice truly acceptable to the Father. Christ's offering brings about the covenant of the new People of God. Thus its reality requires the response of creation. The response is not a passivity—a mere reception of God's gifts of grace. The response is an active participation in the sacrifice that effects redemption. It is Mary who gives the first and definitive response. Her response makes her the mother of the faithful. Her response is a compassion with Christ as she fulfills the feminine responsibility for the New Covenant. Pope Benedict XV teaches:

> To such an extent did she suffer and almost die with her suffering and dying Son, and to such an extent did she surrender her maternal rights over her Son for man's salvation, and immolated Him, insofar as she could, in order to appease the justice of God, that we may rightly say that she redeemed the human race together with Christ.[15]

Pope Pius XII in the conclusion of his encyclical *Mystici Corporis* states:

> It was she, the second Eve, who, free from all sin, original or personal, and always more intimately united with her Son, offered Him on Golgotha to the Eternal Father for all

---

15. Pope Benedict XV, Commemorative Letter to the Confraternity of Our Lady of Good Death *Inter Sodalicia* (March 22, 1918) in *Mary in the Documents of the Church*, ed. Paul F. Palmer (Westminster, MD: The Newman Press, 1952), 97.

the children of Adam, sin-stained by his unhappy fall, and her mother's rights and her mother's love were included in the holocaust. Thus she who, according to the flesh, was mother of our Head, through the added title of pain and glory became, according to the Spirit, the mother of all His members [16]

At Calvary Mary is not a passive onlooker. The crucifixion of her Son is not something that just "happens" to her. Mary actively participates in the sacrifice by offering up her Son. It is a mother's sacrifice; the sacrifice of the New Eve. Her sacrifice is different from Christ's but is in covenantal union with it. Without her sacrifice the new creation would not be established. Mary's offering up of Christ is the fulfillment of her "fiat" as the New Eve to the New Adam. This offer is specific to feminine responsibility for the faith. The New Eve held Christ in her womb, but her motherhood in bringing forth the Head resides equally in letting Him go. The mother of Christ must let Him be the Savior. Louis Bouyer states:

> The final gesture, the most sublime perhaps, that a mother has to make is to renounce possession of her child's life, to accept that it should be lived on its own terms. With Mary, this renunciation meant accepting that Christ should deliver himself up to his Father's will, that is, to the Cross. [17]

THE RESPONSE OF MARY, THE RESPONSE OF MAN

The New Covenant could not have been formed without cooperation coming from the side of man. If nothing else, the "fiat" of Mary demonstrates this. The response that Mary gives at Calvary is the feminine response of God's graced creation to the sacrificial love of

16. Pope Pius XII, Encyclical Letter On the Mystical Body of Christ *Mystici Corporis Christi* (June 29, 1943), no. 110.

17. Louis Bouyer, *Seat of Wisdom* (New York: Pantheon Books, 1960), 162–3.

the New Adam. At Calvary, Mary is not simply an individual person whose response to and participation in the Passion of her Son begins and ends with her. Mary represents the Church, the collectivity of the redeemed. The Church is the covenantal partner in redemption: the Body and Bride of Christ.

Because Mary gives her consent to the Cross and offers Christ upon it, the faithful are represented by her. In other words, Mary really can stand in for them because she is their mother. In Mary the entire reality of the faithful is present at Calvary.

Because Mary is the New Eve of the Protogospel, the covenantal partner of Christ, she is the origin of a new humanity. This new humanity, born from the covenant between Christ and Mary, has Mary as its model and mode of existence. The motherhood of Mary and the motherhood of the Church partakes of the same reality. The Church comes from the maternal yes of Mary to the salvific mission of her Son and exists within this reality. Mary's graced response to Christ produces a New People. She has other children born in the likeness of the "firstborn of all creation."

The order of redemption is the relation of the Head and the Body; their covenantal one-flesh union. The Church is not Christ. While the Church is the Mystical Body of Christ, this doesn't mean that she is simply a mere continuation in a monadic fashion of the Incarnation. The Mystical Body of Christ is the consequence of the head/body relation bound together in a free unity. If anything, the Church is the continuation of Mary. The Church is her feminine reality extended in history. Her yes is an authoritative life-giving word. In Mary we see the utter indispensability of feminine responsibility for the faith. Without woman the covenant of redemption would not be fulfilled.

5

THE CHURCH FATHERS AND WOMEN'S AUTHORITY

Mel Gibson's 2004 film *The Passion of the Christ* is arguably the most theologically informed cinematic treatment of Jesus. Gibson based much of the movie on the writings of Blessed Ann Catherine Emmerich, and the film is definitely influenced by a theology rooted in the Protogospel of Genesis 3:15. The film is remarkable for a number of reasons, not the least of which is its unprecedented highly developed mariology. Mary is presented as the covenantal partner of Christ in the accomplishment of His work of redemption. Consistent with Mary's role at the wedding at Cana, Mary enables, encourages, and strengthens Christ in the fulfillment of His mission, and is contrasted with the sinister figure of Satan who throughout the movie seeks to deter Christ from doing the will of the Father.

There are no less than four scenes in which Mary is shown to be the advocate of Christ's Passion.[1] She is not simply a passive observer of Her Son's suffering. She actually helps lead Christ to the Cross. As one example, many viewers of the film find particularly stirring the climactic scene where Christ on the Via Dolorosa (Latin, meaning "Way of Sorrow" or "Path of Sorrow"), His body spent with suffering and overcome by the weight of the Cross, falls to the ground. At this

---

1. Monica Migliorino Miller, *The Theology of the Passion of the Christ* (Staten Is., New York: Alba House, 2005). For a full discussion of the role of Mary in the Gibson film, see pages 13–29.

point a flashback takes place. We see the boy Jesus, who while running, also falls to the ground. A younger Mary rushes to Him and comforts Him. Shifting back to the present moment on the Via Dolorosa, Mary understands her role and rushes to her collapsed Son. She embraces Him and declares, "I am here." By these words and by her abiding maternal presence, Christ is strengthened. His hand reaches out to touch His mother's face and He announces to her, "See Mother, I make all things new." Christ can now summon all His strength and, bearing the Cross, continues on His way to Calvary. Indeed, if the viewer watches closely, one sees Mary raise up her hand as if she were helping Her Son to rise and continue His Passion.

Gibson's *The Passion of the Christ* is shot through with a co-redemptrix theme as Mary exercises her divinely given maternal prerogatives. In this chapter we will examine closely how feminine responsibility for the covenant is recognized and promoted going back to the earliest stages of the tradition—namely, the Fathers of the Church.

One might think that the Church Fathers are the absolute last place to look for any positive statements on the authority of women. Mary Daly indicted the Church of misogyny in her book *The Church and the Second Sex* by copiously quoting the Fathers on the nature of women. Rosemary Radford Ruether totally rejects the New Eve theology of St. Irenaeus, even though it is one of the most positive views of women taught by any Church Father. But for Ruether, the teaching that Mary is the New Eve is still "theology on male terms" because this theology scapegoats women as the cause of sin in the world and promotes what she believes is a male tendency to divide spirit from matter.[2]

The Church Fathers (those great bishops and theologians of the first five hundred years of Christianity) are a special target of femi-

---

2. Rosemary Radford Ruether, *Sexism and God–talk* (Boston: Beacon Press, 1983), 151–2.

nist rage, and it must be admitted that these early Church thinkers are certainly not well known for their support for women's liberation. It must be acknowledged that most of the Church Fathers were heavily influenced by Neoplatonism, a radically dualist philosophy that associates men with good and women with evil. Men represent spiritual realities, God, the soul, the intellect,—realities that are permanent and unchanging—thus good. Evil is all that has fallen away from the spiritual realm, namely, the earth and material existence. Women, by their nature, are on the side of this fallen realm. There can never be an inherent peace between the two realms. If anything, they are inherently antagonistic. In a perfect world all human beings would be male. Better yet, there would be no sex at all. The fact of sexual difference is the first and most primary indication that something is wrong with the world. In Platonic thought, a world filled with difference is fragmented. It is a world that has ceased to have unity because it is fallen from the One, the monist realm of spiritual unity in which the fragmentation of temporal existence is swallowed, including sexual differentiation.

Order in such a disunified and antagonistic world is achieved through domination and suppression by the superior male force over the inferior female force. The elimination of chaos is accomplished by the rational male's control over the irrational female. And so this totally false and unnecessary battle of the sexes continues even to the present day.

The Fathers of the Church lived in a time dominated by a pagan philosophy whose degrading view of women was confronted by the faith of the Church which, according to its sacramental and moral life, teaches that men and women share an equal dignity and are partners in redemption. In the writings of the Fathers, Greek philosophy is not obscuring Christian revelation; rather, it is the Church's revolutionary teaching that is slowly and painfully displacing the dominant philosophical view that women are inferior to men. When the Fathers base their writings on the revelation of Christ, a view of women begins to emerge that recognizes their essential role in the fulfillment of the world's redemption in Christ. This redemption is dependent upon women, a dependency that is rooted in the created goodness of women as such.

St. Augustine taught that the salvation of the world was historically accomplished by a covenant between Christ and Mary. Indeed, Augustine defends the honor of Mary against the heretics of his day who deny the goodness of the body and the female sex. The Gnostics denied that God in Christ could or would have anything to do with a woman, much less be conceived and given birth to by one! Such a thing was utterly scandalous to them, but not so for Augustine:

> Those likewise are to be detested who deny that our Lord Jesus Christ had Mary as his mother on earth. That dispensation did honor to both sexes male and female, and showed that both had a part in God's care; not only that which he assumed, but that also through which he assumed it, being a man born of a woman.[3]

There is no indication that one sex is superior to the other. The fact that God entered human history as a male does not mean the male sex is superior. St. Augustine clearly teaches that through the Incarnation God honors both sexes. Moreover, both sexes are actively involved in the world's redemption. It is important to note that St. Augustine is not afraid to affirm that Christ is dependent on Mary.

For St. Augustine, the Church is the New Eve. His teaching affirms that femininity is part of the order of redemption. Augustine's exegesis on Psalm 127 states that salvation is centered on a pair: Christ and His Church. This is a nuptial pair, as Christ and His

---

3. St. Augustine, *Faith and the Creed*, IV, 9, trans. John H.S. Burleigh, *Augustine: Earlier Writings*, Library of Christian Classics, Vol. 6 (Philadelphia: The Westminster Press, 1953), 358.

Church are prefigured in the first couple. Augustine specifically affirms this in the beautiful way he parallels the divinely induced sleep of Adam with the sleep of death Christ experienced on the Cross, from whose pierced side came the Church, the New Eve (quoted in chapter two).[4]

As regards the authority of women, it is important to note that Christ is not effecting salvation alone. Salvation is effected through the Church, His Bride, who exemplifies all that is feminine. In Augustine's theology there is a sense in which the feminine Church is a co-cause of salvation. The Church, for instance, gives birth to Christ's children. Eve, who bore children in suffering, is the sign of the Church who will bear children spiritually. The Church bears children specifically as Christ's Bride. As a mother she suffers over her children, groaning over them. In this way, the Church is the true "Mother of all the living" who looks forward to the time when her children shall rise from the dead and all "pain and groaning shall pass away."[5]

THE EQUALITY OF WOMEN

St. Augustine does not disparage what is feminine. Indeed, salvation is accomplished through the feminine. His theology at least implies that an equal dignity exists between the male Christ and the female Church. This is, of course, the "whole Christ," the *Christus totus*, the Head and the Body, *sponsus* and *sponsa*.

St. Jerome also taught that the female sex participates in a special way in the order of redemption—in a way that is equal in importance and dignity to the male existence of Christ. In St. Jerome's letter to Eustochiam it is clear that salvation is dependent on a woman. The "rod of Jesse" is the Virgin Mary. The flower of the rod is

---

4. St. Augustine, *Psalm 127*, 4, *Nicene and Post-Nicene Fathers,* Vol. 8 (Grand Rapids, MI: Wm. B. Eerdmans), 607 (PL 37.1672, Ps 126,7).

5. Ibid., 608.

Jesus.[6] The passage speaks of a certain equivalence between Christ and His mother in terms of their common humanity, and Jerome implies that Christ is dependent upon the human Mary. Furthermore, Christ alone does not exemplify virginity. Christ and His mother share the dignity of virginity in an equal fashion as Jerome writes: "For me virginity is consecrated in the persons of Mary and Christ."[7] Furthermore, Jerome does not hesitate to say that Mary in her fruitful virginity is like God Himself because she conceived and gave life without a loss of her purity.

St. Irenaeus, as no other Church Father, developed a theology of Mary as the New Eve. In *Against Heresies* Irenaeus very explicitly teaches that salvation is accomplished by a woman. The bodily presence of Christ is dependent on the body of Mary.[8] Christ is the New Adam only through the obedience of the New Eve:

> For inasmuch as He has a pre-existence as a saving Being, it was necessary that what might be saved should also be called into existence, in order that the being who saves should not exist in vain.

In accordance with this design, Mary the Virgin is found obedient, saying, "Behold the handmaid of the Lord; be it done unto me according to thy word."[9] Mary's obedience does not mean that she is just God's passive instrument. Mary's yes is causative of salvation as Eve's disobedience was the source of man's damnation. Irenaeus teaches:

> But Eve was disobedient; for she did not obey when as yet a virgin. And even as she, having indeed a husband, Adam,

---

6. St. Jerome, *Letter 22 to Eustochiam*, 19, trans. W.H. Fremantle, Nicene and Post-Nicene Fathers, Vol. 6 (Grand Rapids, MI: Wm. B. Eerdmans), 29.

7. Ibid., 18, p. 29.

8. St. Irenaeus, *Against Heresies*, XXII, 2, Ante-Nicene Fathers, Vol. 1, (Grand Rapids, MI: Wm. B. Eerdmans, 1967), 454 (PG 7, 1.255–256).

9. Ibid., XXII, 4, p. 455 (PG 7, 1.258–259).

but being nevertheless as yet a virgin . . . was made the cause of death, both to herself and to the entire human race; so also did Mary, having a man betrothed [to her], and being nevertheless a virgin, by yielding obedience, became the cause of salvation, both to herself, and the whole human race.[10]

Traditionally, blame for the Fall is attributed to Eve, and thus women are essentially credited for everything having gone wrong. It should be noted, however, that embedded into this accusation is a testimony to the importance of female power—that a woman even had the power to cause everything to go wrong. The story of the Fall is not about Satan going after the "weaker sex" to bring about universal rebellion against the kingdom of God. Actually, Satan focuses his attention on the gender that, by her nuptial and maternal life-giving power, is the moral force that holds the world together. Genesis teaches it is the woman who brings to an end the frontier of solitude: the "not good" of human isolation and alienation, the antithesis of authentic human living. By the creation of the woman the male knows himself and is enabled to fulfill his identity. Thus the perfect strategy for Satan is to attack the heart of human communion. If Eve falls, creation falls with her.

Satan attacks not the weak link of humanity, but the link that holds humanity together. In any case, Genesis 3:6 reads: "So she took some of its fruit and ate it; and she also gave some to her husband, who was with her, and he ate it" (NAB). He was "with her." Adam is not a Johnny-come-lately to the devil's seduction. Adam is "with her." Also notice that the next verse states, "Then the eyes of both were opened . . ." It is not as if Eve fell first and then Adam after. The text clearly states, "*Then* the eyes *of both* were opened, and they knew

---

10. Ibid.

that they were naked." They are one flesh. Their fall is simultaneous. On Eve's inducement, they rise and fall together.

The early Fathers do not reject the feminine as something unworthy of serving as God's vehicle of grace, as woman is at the very center of the Fall. Rather, woman is placed at the very center of salvation according to God's design for the Incarnation. Mary's consent to become the Mother of God undoes the cords of death forged by Eve's disobedience. Through a woman grace bursts forth into the world. In this way Mary is a co-redemptrix with Christ.

Pagans of St. Augustine's time, whose thinking was dominated by a pessimistic dualism, utterly rejected any idea that the human body would rise from the dead and participate in salvation. And most certainly the female body, so tied to the earth and far from the spiritual power of God, would not rise from the dead. St. Augustine, whom feminist theologians especially hate among the Fathers, defended the female body as being nature not vice. Being nature, it is made by God and thus it is good. The female body is not only nature but it has sacramental value: the woman from the beginning of creation prefigured the Church in union with Christ. God created both the man and the woman. "He then, who created both sexes will restore both."[11]

As God "built up" Eve from the rib of Adam, Christ builds up His Church. For Augustine, a woman's body stands for the Body of Christ. Christ has built this Body, and the unity between Him and the Church is marital, prefigured by the marriage between Adam and Eve. Augustine's theology of the resurrection of the body rests on the sexually symbolic meaning of the body. This meaning was first given in Adam and Eve. It is finally and ultimately fulfilled when the body is raised from the dead. Augustine breaks with Neoplatonism when he unequivocally affirms that the significance of gender is not erased

---

11. St. Augustine, City of God, XXII, 17, trans. Marcus Dods, *The Works of Aurelius Augustine*, Bishop of Hippo, Vol. 2, (Edinburgh: T & T Clark, 1878), 509–10 (CSEL 40.625).

in the eschaton. Redemption means that both sexes, imbued with religious meaning, shall be raised up.

THE MARITAL AUTHORITY OF WOMEN

St. Augustine's teaching demonstrates that the equality of man and woman is part of the Church's tradition. The Fathers assert this truth despite their Neoplatonic tendencies, and the Fathers teach that women contribute to and are a necessary part of what it means for the world to be saved. The authority of women is recognized especially in the covenant of marriage. The Fathers upheld the woman's right to consent to marriage at a time when women had very few rights regarding marriage. Like men, women too should be free to choose her vocation in response to God's call. A woman could not be compelled by her family or even by her father to marry if it were against her will. St. Clement of Alexandria taught that a man could not force a woman to marry him or love him.[12] In his work *Concerning Virgins*, St. Ambrose supported the Roman law which allowed women to choose their own husbands and the freedom of a woman to choose perpetual virginity. He also severely criticized the dowry system because it treated women like merchandise to be sold for a price. He stated, "Slaves are sold under more tolerable conditions" and possess more dignity, as they can often choose their own masters, but if a "maiden chooses it is an offense, if not an insult."[13]

The freedom and authority of women is most clearly defended by the Fathers in their choice to be a consecrated virgin. Young women were even instructed to defy their angry parents. They were not to be concerned about losing the security of their home or their father's

---

12. St. Clement of Alexandria, *The Stromata, II*, 23, *The Ante-Nicene Fathers*, Vol. 2, (Grand Rapids, MI: Wm. B. Eerdmans, 1956), 377 (PG 8.1087).

13. St. Ambrose, *Concerning Virgins*, I, 9, 56, trans. H. De Romestin, *The Nicene and Post-Nicene Fathers*, Vol. 10, Second series, (Grand Rapids, MI: Wm. B. Eerdmans, 1955), 372 (PL 16.215).

inheritance.[14] In St. Jerome's letter to Eustochium he taught that consecrated virginity by God's own design is something that can only be freely given. Therefore mothers should not hold their daughters back from this choice. Indeed, the daughter's vow bestowed a new status on her mother as she becomes "now the mother-in-law of God."[15] The freedom and authority to choose consecrated virginity has its preeminent model in Mary. Such a choice could never be imposed.[16]

The Christian teaching on marriage as a sign of the New Covenant requires personal freedom. The radical insight of the Christian faith in the time of the Fathers was that the woman's free consent was as necessary to the validity of the marriage bond as was her husband's. The bride's consent, equally with the man's, entered into the causality of the sacramental sign. The free consent of the spouse is necessary for the exercise of conjugal rights: that is, the authority spouses possess over one another's body. Because marital authority is mutual, the ban on divorce was equally binding on the husband as well as the wife. St. Augustine recognized that the mutual authority spouses have over one another's bodies is the foundation of marital equality.[17] For example, based on 1 Corinthians 7:4, Augustine teaches that a husband could not make a vow of perpetual continence without the consent of his wife.[18]

Women exercise tremendous authority over their husbands in the area of fidelity. First of all, there can be no double standard. In contrast to the surrounding culture, Christian marriage demanded

14. Ibid., 1, 11, 63, p. 373 (PL 16.217).

15. St. Jerome, *Eustochiam*, 20 (CSEL 54.170).

16. St. Augustine, *On Virginity*, IV, 4, trans. John McQuade, S.M., *Fathers of the Church*, Vol. 27, (New York: Fathers of the Church, Inc. 1955), 147 (CSEL 41–42.238).

17. St. Augustine, *Sermon on the Mount*, I, 16, 43, trans. Denis J. Kavanagh, *Fathers of the Church*, Vol. 11 (New York: Fathers of the Church, Inc., 1951), 65 (CCL 35.49).

18. St. Augustine, *The Good of Marriage*, 6, trans. Charles T. Wilcox, *Fathers of the Church*, Vol. 27, (New York: Fathers of the Church, Inc., 1955), 17 (CSEL 41–42.195).

complete fidelity, not only from wives but from husbands too! In Augustine's sermon *To the Married* he is adamant that wives not tolerate infidelity from their spouses.[19] Augustine tells Christian husbands that they are under the guardianship of their wives. And he says to the wives:

> Do not allow your husbands to fornicate! Hurl the Church herself against them! Obstruct them, not through the law courts, not through the procounsel . . . not even through the Emperor, but through Christ. . . . The wife has not authority over her body, but the husband. Why do men exalt? Listen to what follows. The husband likewise has not authority over his body, but the wife. . . . Despise all things for love of your husband. But seek that he be chaste and call him to account if his chastity be amiss. . . . Who would tolerate an adulterous wife? Is the woman enjoined to tolerate an adulterous husband? . . . Those of you who are chaste women, however, do not imitate your wanton husbands. May this be far from you. May they either live with you or perish alone. A woman owes her modesty not to a wanton husband but to God and to Christ.[20]

St. Augustine actually teaches that wives can call their husbands "to account" if they fail in chastity. The wife is not to tolerate adulterous behavior. A woman has authority to call her husband to live up to the responsibilities of the marriage covenant. St. Augustine sees specific biblical warrant for female authority in the area of chastity, which he taught is one of the three goods of marriage. Along with the goods of children and indissolubility, it is of the essence of the marital bond. The wife has authority to require her husband to live up

19. St. Augustine, Sermon 392, "*To the Married*," trans. Quincy Howe, Jr., *Selected Sermons of St. Augustine* (New York: Holt, Rinehart and Winston, 1966), 32–3 (PL 39.1711–1712).

20. Ibid.

to these goods, but certainly her authority covers any of his spousal duties. A wife is not only there to serve her spouse. A wife's vocation means she has the authority to call her spouse to serve her and their children in his vocation as husband and father. She has authority to call him to live up to his end of their one-flesh union. The wife has authority to call her husband to do what is good for their marital bond, and vice versa. This is the true sense of male and female authority. Equality does not mean that the man and woman have the same responsibilities. They don't. But the man and the woman have an equal authority to lead each other to fulfill the vocations God has called them to according to the meaning of their sexuality.

There are certain passages of St. Paul that talk about authority and submission. In today's Church influenced by feminist thinking, these passages are not at all popular. In fact, they are often edited by lectors during Mass so as not to offend the women in the congregation. The passages are Colossians 3:18–20 and Ephesians 5:22–32. Both passages start out with the thorny teaching that wives should be submissive to their husbands. The Letter to the Ephesians states:

> Wives, be subject to your husbands, as to the Lord. For the husband is the head of the wife as Christ is the head of the Church, his body, and is himself its Savior. As the Church is subject to Christ, so let wives also be subject in everything to their husbands. Husbands, love your wives, as Christ loved the Church and gave himself up for her, that he might sanctify her, having cleansed her by the washing of water with the word, that he might present the Church to himself in splendor, without spot or wrinkle or any such thing, that she might be holy and without blemish. Even so husbands should love their wives as their own bodies. He who loves his wife loves himself. For no man ever hates his own flesh, but nourishes and cherishes it, as Christ does the Church,

because we are members of his body. "For this reason a man shall leave his father and mother and be joined to this wife, and the two shall become one flesh." This is a great mystery, and I mean in reference to Christ and the Church. (Eph 5:22–32)

No one likes the idea of submission. Pride rebels against it and it is possible that being submissive could lead to exploitation. In our day and age it is believed that one who is submissive lacks dignity. Such a person is giving up his rights and permitting himself or herself to be oppressed. Submission is for slaves, not free people. It is to be avoided at all costs. Yet women are told precisely that they are the ones who are supposed to be submissive, and to their husbands no less! Many modern exegetes simply dismiss these Pauline verses as historically conditioned. They argue that at the time St. Paul was writing, submissiveness was a women's lot and the Apostle is merely articulating this outdated ethic. Since women had no authority, the only thing they could do was be submissive. Authority was solely in the hands of men, and thus male authority is equated with power: the evil power of patriarchy.

The Pauline passages on the submission of wives to their husbands are dismissed out of hand. It is believed that these verses have no theological importance. This is a huge mistake. These passages should not be cut with the feminist razor. Rather they should be understood according to the real meaning of authority. Not only are we in desperate need of a good theology of submission, but we are in need of a good theology of male authority based on the teaching of Ephesians 5. Yes, wives are instructed to be submissive to their husbands because the husband is head of his wife as Christ is Head of the Church. But the husband is also instructed to love his wife. What does love mean but to give oneself over to another? The husband is to give up himself for his wife as Christ gave Himself up for the Church.

This is a form of submission, a form as deep and as equally serious as the submission of wives. The husband's submission to his wife is the only way her submission could be possible or make any sense. In the Christian religion, obedience and submission to another's authority is never due to tyranny or despotism. We are talking about the love and the covenant between persons that respect human freedom and are made possible because of that freedom.

If the passage is historically conditioned, it is so only to the extent that the author bluntly states the duty of the wife. Female submission was nothing new to the culture of the time. What was new—and entirely changes the meaning of feminine submission—is St. Paul's instruction to husbands. St. Pope John Paul II calls the teaching of Ephesians the "Gospel 'innovation'" because, for the first time, the truth about men and women is revealed. A mutual submission exists between spouses.[21] The wife is not to submit to a spouse who is her master, who lords his authority over her. Not at all! He is instructed to give himself up for her. In the Christian dispensation, husbands are expected to do something entirely new based on the example of Christ and the sacramental role of the husband in making Christ real in the world. They are to fully serve their wives instead of women simply serving and obeying them. The most profound submission is to die for another. When a person dies for another, he or she has truly submitted themselves to this other person. They have spent themselves for the good of the other.

Notice that the instruction to wives on being submissive to their husbands is not unqualified. They should be submissive to them "as if to the Lord." The instruction has a context. Submission is based on the one flesh of the spouses in which it is presupposed that husbands will love their wives as Christ loves His Church. The wife also has authority. She is the body of her husband, as verses 28–29 state. As the body is in a one-flesh unity with the head, she can and must call

---

21. *Mulieris Dignitatem*, no. 24.

her husband to do what the head is supposed to do in the fulfillment
of this one-flesh unity that is a living sacrament of Christ and the
Church. Husbands and wives do not have authority over one another
for the sake of exercising power. If this were the case, their relation
would be one of constant tension and disharmony. Authority and
submission exists to create a one-flesh unity. It is there to serve the
bond. It is exercised for the good of the bond, so that the marriage
will be a good marriage, so that the spouses can do what is good for
their marriage together. The person who exercises authority does not
do so for the sake of being served. It is exercised so that his and her
marriage may be served.

What does all this authority and submission mean in practical terms? Let me give some examples. If the wife is in the habit
of spending money in a manner that is detrimental to the family
budget, her husband can require that she cease doing so, and she
should obey. If a husband is lazy and does not want to work and so
is neglecting his duty towards his wife and children, his wife can
require that he get a job, and he should obey. If the husband or the
wife is abusing alcohol or drugs, the abuser should be obedient to the
spouse who requires that he/she seek proper treatment to overcome
this destructive behavior. If a spouse is doing something immoral
like using contraception or cheating on the income tax, the other
spouse can and should exercise their authority and require that this
immoral behavior cease.

It is really quite wrong to edit the unpopular passages in Colossians and Ephesians that speak of submission. First of all, the teaching on women's submission is the Word of God. Today, the verses
are censored because they are interpreted negatively according to the
dictates of feminist ideology. Instead they should be interpreted posi-
tively from the perspective of faith and an insightful theology that is
able to articulate the full dimensions of submission, which includes
that of the husband whose love is placed at the service of his wife

and children. Many liturgists would rather respond to this Scripture according to a political knee-jerking that is utterly unable to see the theological importance of the teaching for marriage and its enduring moral value. Its value ought not be suppressed according to whatever political viewpoint is in vogue.

Liturgists are not setting the Holy Spirit free from the bonds of patriarchy when they edit out passages on women's submission. They are stifling the Holy Spirit. It is probable that, at any given time within the context of the Eucharist, a woman may need to hear the virtue of submission preached to her for the sake of doing what is good and right for her marriage. Upon hearing these words a wife may realize that in some specific matter that affects her husband she has been acting selfishly or pridefully. She may also need to hear of how her husband is exhorted to give himself up for her—a love which makes her submission possible. And a husband may need to hear that he is to love his wife. Marital love is submission to another.

St. Caesarius of Arles upheld the moral equality of Christian men and women. Men and women are redeemed equally by Christ's blood and so a double standard cannot exist.[22] In contrast to the Gnostics, female sexuality is not at all a hindrance to salvation. This patristic teaching alone makes the Fathers revolutionary for their time. In contrast to the conventional wisdom of the age, men have no special spiritual place. God does not view them as privileged. They do not have a greater capacity for salvation than women.

St. John Chrysostom taught that women had authority to instruct, advise, and admonish their husbands in the moral life. Consider the following excerpts from one of his homilies:

Indeed nothing—nothing, I repeat—is more potent than a good and prudent woman in molding a man and shaping his soul in whatever way she desires. For he will not bear

---

22. St. Caesarius, *Sermon 43*, 3, trans. Sr. Mary Magdelene Mueller, *Fathers of the Church*, Vol. 31 (New York: Fathers of the Church, Inc., 1956), 215 (CSEL 103.191).

with friends, or teachers, or magistrates in the same way as with his wife, when she admonishes and advises him. Her admonition carries with it a kind of pleasure, because of his very great love of the one who is admonishing him. . . . She is devoted to him in all things and is closely bound to him as the body is fastened to the head. . . .

Therefore, I beseech women to carry this out in practice and to give their husbands only the proper advice. For, just as a woman has great power for good, so also she has it for evil. A woman destroyed Absalom; a woman destroyed Amnon; a woman would have destroyed Job; a woman saved Nabel from being murdered; a woman saved an entire nation.

Furthermore, Deborah and Judith and innumerable other women directed the success of men who were generals. And that is why Paul said: 'For how dost thou know, O wife, whether thou wilt save thy husband?' In this way too we see Persis, Mary and Priscilla sharing in the Apostles' difficult trials. You also ought to imitate these women, and mold the character of your husbands, not only by your words but also by your example. . . .

But when you provide him with instruction, not only by your words but also by your example, then he will both show approval of you and be the more effectively convinced.[23]

The passage is full of statements that speak of feminine authority. We are told that women are to "mold" men and "shape" their souls. Wives are to "admonish" and "advise" their husbands. They have authority to mold the character of their husbands and give them instruction. When St. John Chrysostom talks of Deborah and Judith,

---

23. St. John Chrysostom, *Homily 61*, trans. Sr. Thomas Aquinas Goggin, *Fathers of the Church*, Vol. 41 (New York: Fathers of the Church, Inc., 1960), 161–2 (PG 59.340–341).

we see that women have the power to direct the destiny of men. Men who are in positions of authority are directed to success or failure by women. A wife even has the power to save her husband from damnation. Evidently, if wives can instruct their husbands, husbands have a duty to obey.

St. John Chrysostom does not fail to indicate the marital foundation of male and female authority. A wife can and should teach her husband, because she is bound to him as the body to the head. The essence of marriage is the basis for the proper exercise of authority and obedience. The authority of husbands and wives is moral and sacramental, and therefore has as its aim the spouses' salvation. It is a moral authority based on a bond of love.

St. Paulinus of Nola teaches that a wife's moral leadership is a sign of God's marriage with the Church:

> Your wife, who does not lead her husband to effeminacy or greed, but brings you back to self-discipline and courage to become the bones of her husband, is worthy of admiration because of her great emulation of God's marriage with the Church.[24]

Taking his cues from the second chapter of Genesis, St. Paulinus refers to a wife as the very bones of her husband. Bones give shape and structure to bodies which would otherwise collapse. They give bodies strength and cause them to stand erect. Adam declares that Eve is "bone of my bones and flesh of my flesh" (Gen 2:23). Paulinus uses the verse to describe what a good wife does for her husband. In building up his moral life she builds him up as husband.

The Church Fathers constantly praise women for their superior practice of Christian virtue. Female sexuality is not at all an obstacle

---

24. St. Paulinus of Nola, *Letter 44*, 94, trans. P.G. Walsh, *Letters of St. Paulinis of Nola*, Ancient Christian Writers, Vol. 26 (Westminster, MD: The Newman Press, 1967), 237 (CSEL 29.372).

to holiness, and in many cases it is an aid. St. Augustine, in his treatise *On Virginity*, taught that Thecla and Chrispina were models of
discipleship. Matthew 20:22 is addressed to male disciples and connects discipleship with the ability to drink from the cup of Christ's
Passion. Augustine believes women have equal strength to drink
from this cup as well.[25] St. Cyprian taught that women martyrs were
stronger than their male torturers.[26] St. Ambrose praises a female
martyr for having kept her chastity from abuse by men.[27] Eusebius
records the martyrdom of Blandina who, before her own death, gives
encouragement to the men who are to follow her.[28] The Fathers consider Mary Magdalene the preeminent model of penitence for men as
well as women.[29]

WOMEN AND THE CONSECRATED LIFE

The Fathers of the Church are unanimous in their respect for women
who choose a life of consecrated virginity. St. Jerome exalts women
because they are favored with this vocation more frequently than
men.[30] The early Fathers taught that female virginity was a unique
charism with a special significance that male virginity lacked. The
female virgin was a living sign of the Church. St. Jerome states: "As-
suredly no gold or silver vessel was ever so dear to God as is the
temple of a virgin's body. The shadow went before, but now the reality has come."[31] A consecrated virgin makes the maritally-based
redemption of Christ real in the world. St. Jerome called the con-

25. St. Augustine, *On Virginity*, 44, 45, p. 199 (CSEL 41–42.289–290).

26. St. Cyprian, *On the Dress of Virgins*, 6, trans. Roy J. Deferrari, The Fathers of
the Church, Vol. 36 (New York: The Fathers of the Church, Inc., 1958), 36–7 (CSEL
3,1.192).

27. St. Ambrose, *Concerning Virgins*, II, 4, 22, p. 377 (PL 16.224).

28. Eusebius, *Ecclesiastical History*, 5, 1 (PG 20.426).

29. St. Paulinus of Nola, *Letter* 23, 39 & 42 (CSEL 29.195, 197).

30. St. Jerome, *Eustochiam*, 21, p. 30 (CSEL 54.173).

31. Ibid., 23, p. 31 (CSEL 54.175–176).

secrated virgin a bride. Virgins are like Mary. Indeed, consecrated virgins are another Mary. Virgins give birth to the spirit of Christ's salvation which they "have wrought upon the earth."[32]

It is not hard to see women's great dignity and place in the Church. A virgin, precisely because of the nuptial meaning of her body, causes the salvation of Christ to be present. The presence of Christ's redemption is "wrought" by these women. It is their work.

St. Augustine also taught that virgins exemplify the Church. Virgins deserve great honor because they preserve in their flesh what the whole Church preserves by her faith. The Church, imitating Mary, is a bride and mother. The Church is both virgin and mother. The Church is a virgin because she keeps the faith intact. She is a mother because she gives birth in the Spirit to the children of Christ. The Church's holiness exists in those female members who make real in themselves the Church's physical and spiritual holiness.[33] Consecrated virgins preserve in their own flesh the espousal of the Church to Christ. In this way woman, indeed the female body, is a sign of redemption.

St. Ambrose made a comparison between the consecrated virgin and the Church. He emphasized the symbolic value of the virgin as a sign of the Church's motherhood. The Church, while remaining a virgin, gives birth to many offspring. Like Mary, the Church bears children not by the power of men but by the power of the Spirit.[34]

The Church today could benefit greatly by going back and emphasizing these insights of the Fathers regarding the symbolic role of women. It is thought, even among those who cannot identify with the feminist point of view, that priestly authority is the only authority, priestly office the only office. It is mistakenly believed that unless women become priests they are doomed by patriarchy to remain

32. Ibid., 38, p. 39 (CSEL 54.204).
33. St. Augustine, On Virginity, II, 2, p. 145 (CSEL 41.236).
34. St. Ambrose, Concerning Virgins, I, 6, 31, p. 368 (PL 16.208).

invisible. How wrong this is! Such a conclusion about women in the Church is the fruit of a monist philosophy about power. Even the Church Fathers, despite all their Neoplatonism, escaped this deadly perspective. Authority is maritally exercised. The authority of man and woman, if real, share in and make present the authority of the one-flesh love of Christ and the Church. If we keep this in mind, as Christians we will come to understand that the authority of the male priest, because it is first Eucharistic, is authority put to the service of the female Church—the Body of Christ whose only true and appropriate sign is woman.

6

THE AUTHORITY OF WOMEN

Having just completed my Master's degree in Theology at Loyola University in the early 1980s, I landed a position teaching religion to teenage girls at a high school in Chicago. The school, operated by the Franciscan Sisters of Lemont, Illinois, was called Madonna—named of course for the Mother of Christ. I patronized the Chicago transit system before I was able to afford my silver 1978 Toyota Celica to conveniently speed me around the city. Thus five days a week, starting from Rogers Park on the far northeast side of town, I took an L train and two buses to the corner of Belmont and Pulaski at the northwest side of town where the school was located. If nothing else, the trek afforded me time to read books. One day, however, while I was absorbed in the *Rise and Fall of the Third Reich*, the Belmont Avenue bus came to one of its endless stops. A woman got on whom, though the seat across the aisle was completely empty, opted to sit down next to me. Even though I was obviously engrossed in a literally weighty book, she wanted to talk. Noticing that I had a briefcase she said, "Oh, you must be a business woman or a professor or something."

I said, "No, I'm a high school teacher."

"No kidding. What high school?"

I replied, "Madonna High School for Girls."

Then she said, "Wow, they actually named a school for the pop singer Madonna!"

Of course, that anyone would think that a high school would be named for someone very much unlike the real Madonna is enormously humorous. I have to admit, I had to make a real effort not to laugh. I managed to politely inform the more than mistaken bus rider, "No. The school is a Catholic school named for Mary the Mother of God, not Madonna the singer." To which the embarrassed woman responded, "Of course, yeah, for heaven's sake. How can I be so dumb?"

I hate to say it, but this would not be the last time someone would display the same ignorance regarding the namesake of Madonna High School for Girls. That people would be prone to such error indicates that the culture has definitely been hijacked. When the word *Madonna* is mentioned, it's not Mary who comes to mind but someone arguably her antithesis. A pop singer with the name "Madonna" has managed to rise to the center of consciousness when the word is used in the public square. It's not Christ's mother who comes to mind but a crude and irreverent vocalist. The Queen of Heaven is not recognized as the Queen of this world. This tells us that we have a great deal of work to do to bring the culture back to a true reverence for women and a real awareness of their life-giving authority. Let us now turn to the essence of female authority and its practical exercise by which the world itself is held together.

THE MEANING OF HEADSHIP
IN 1 CORINTHIANS 11:3–16

Feminist theologians consider St. Paul the chief enemy of women's liberation. He instructs women to keep silent, be completely submissive, never exercise authority over men, and suggests that women are more susceptible to deception than men (1 Tim 11–12). If the teaching of St. Paul is interpreted through the monist understanding of power it is no wonder his teaching is offensive to so many modern women. The following passage from St. Paul is regarded as particularly offensive:

> But I want you to understand that the head of every man is Christ, the head of a woman is her husband, and the head of Christ is God. Any man who prays or prophesies with his head covered dishonors his head, but any woman who prays or prophesies with her head unveiled dishonors her head—it is the same as if her head were shaven. For if a woman will not veil herself, then she should cut off her hair; but if it is disgraceful for a woman to be shorn or shaven, let her wear a veil. For a man ought not to cover his head, since he is the image and glory of God; but woman is the glory of man. (For man was not made from woman, but woman from man. Neither was man created for woman, but woman for man.) That is why a woman ought to have a veil on her head, because of the angels. (Nevertheless, in the Lord woman is not independent of man nor man of woman; for as woman was made from man, so man is now born of woman. And all things are from God.) Judge for yourselves; is it proper for a woman to pray to God with her head uncovered? Does not nature itself teach you that for a man to wear long hair is degrading to him, but if a woman has long hair, it is her pride? For her hair is given to her for a covering. If any one is disposed to be contentious, we recognize no other practice, nor do the churches of God. (1 Cor 11:3–16)

Those who advocate women's liberation regard this passage as a prime example of Pauline misogyny.[1] Compared to men it appears that women are placed in a secondary position. Men, after all, im-

---

1. Denise Lardner Carmody, *Biblical Woman: Contemporary Reflections on Scriptural Texts* (New York: Crossroad, 1988), 128–30.

age God, but women are "only" the reflection of men, and men are placed in a position of headship over women. It is a mistake, however, to read this very important passage as if St. Paul were seeking a rationalization for male power. The passage is about the marital/covenantal order of the male and female relation that has for its foundation the Trinitarian relation between the Father and the Son.

First of all, it is important to reemphasize that being a head means being a source. Notice that verse 3 states that Christ is the Head of all males. The Greek word here means "male," and not "mankind" which would include both men and women. Certainly, Christ is the Lord of males and females. So why does St. Paul teach here that Christ is only a head in relation to the masculine sex? How could it be that men are in God's image and women are not, when St. Paul knew very well Genesis 1:27 taught that both males and females are created in the image of God?

It must be, then, that men are the "image and glory of God" in some special way. There must be something shared between God and males. Christ is called the Head of males, while males are the heads of their wives. Christ and men are heads because they are both origins. Notice that even Christ, who is God, is under the headship of someone, namely, the Father (1 Cor 11:3)! He is under the headship of the Father because Christ is *from* the Father, eternally begotten by Him. Christ is the Head of males because there is something about both Christ and males that images God. Christ's headship in relation to males is that of archetype to image. God the Father is the Head of Christ because Christ is His image. Christ is the Head of men because they are His image. Males have a representative sacramental role. They are symbols of Christ. Men have Christ as their Head because the meaning of being male and the meaning of masculine authority are derived from Christ. In this way, men exist as the "image and glory of God" in a way that women do not.

Husbands are the heads of their wives because, at the Beginning, the male served as the origin of woman. Eve is made from the side of Adam. He is her source. The creation of woman from the side of man is the explanation of her being as the Father is the explanation of the Son's being. "As the existence of Christ is given in the existence of God, and as the existence of woman is given in the existence of man, so the existence of man is given in the existence of Christ."[2]

1 Corinthians 11:7 states that women are the glory of men. The man is her source. She is drawn from his side; she is part of his being; she is the male's indispensable complement. Taken from the man she is yet different from him and so she reveals who he is. The woman defines him. The man is completed through the creation of woman: "This at last is bone of my bones and flesh of my flesh; she shall be called Woman, because she was taken out of Man" (Gen 2:23). The authority of headship is derived from being the origin of life to another. The woman is not a head in the sense that the man is, yet she too is a source and thus she too has authority, an authority different from his but in relation to his.

THE WOMAN'S AUTHORITY

The key section in this passage from St. Paul's First Letter to the Corinthians states:

> Nevertheless, in the Lord woman is not independent of man nor man of woman; for as woman was made from man, so man is now born of woman. And all things are from God. (1 Cor 11:11)

We have already seen how male headship is the result of being the origin of woman. Here, St. Paul states the essence of feminine

---

2. C.K. Barrett, *A Commentary on the First Epistle to the Corinthians* (New York: Harper and Row, 1968), 249.

authority: "man is now born of woman." It must be asked at this point, if woman has authority because she is a source in relation to man, then how is it that St. Paul teaches that when a woman prays or prophesies she must wear a veil as a sign of her inferiority? Well, St. Paul does not teach this. All of 1 Corinthians 11:3–16 is focused on the proper order of the marital covenant based on Genesis 2:21–23. The ordering has to do with who came first and who is from whom. It is concerned, not about demonstrating the inferiority of woman, but with sexual differentiation. St. Paul says it is a disgrace for a man to wear his hair long. A woman, on the other hand, must wear a veil. The man's short hair and the woman's veil distinguish them and are ways for them to exalt the created order that is the result of God's wisdom based on sexual differentiation. By wearing a veil the woman sharply and visibly shows her difference.[3] The baptismal equality of man and woman (Gal 3:28) does not erase sexual difference.

Some Bibles translate verse 10 as: "For this reason a woman ought to have a sign of submission on her head because of the angels." This is inaccurate. The Greek word *exousia* does not mean "submission." It means "authority." "For this reason a woman ought to have authority on her head because of the angels." Furthermore, *exousia* is power that is not exercised by someone over someone else. Instead, it is power that a person possesses and exercises in their own right.[4] The Oriental roots of the word give it this meaning. The veil is not a sign of male power over a woman, but a sign of the woman's own power.[5]

The veil is a sign of what feminine power? It is a sign of her ability to worship. The veil is the sign of the woman's liturgical authority. She is covered, which means that she has been brought into God's

---

3. Ibid., 251.

4. Andre Feuillet, "La Dignité et la Rôle de la Femme D Apres Quelques Textes Pauliniens: Comparaison avec L'Ancien Testament," *New Testament Studies*, 21 (1975), 160.

5. William Ramsay, *The Cities of St. Paul: Their Influence on His life and Thought* (Grand Rapids, MI: Baker, 1949), 202ff.

covenant. In the Oriental world, veiling was a sign of honor, not degradation. In the Old Testament, shame is what is uncovered. To go without covering was a sign of harlotry and idolatry (Ezek 16:37). This is certainly expressed in the book of Hosea and is also found in Isaiah 3:24 and Ezekiel 7:18. When God covers His people it is a sign that He is married to them in a covenantal bond. What is the sign that God renounces His people and thus His relation to Israel as her husband? He will "strip her naked and make her as in the day she was born" (Hos 2:3).[6] To be covered has marital/covenantal significance, while being uncovered denotes being outside of the covenant or in violation of it. The veiling of a woman's hair is a liturgical action, as if such covering highlighted or enhanced the significance of her hair. Far from a sign of a woman's inferiority, the veil is a sign of her feminine authority to worship God.[7]

WOMAN, THE COMPLETION OF MAN

The man is head of woman because the man reflects Christ as source and Archetype of the man. But male headship and female authority exists according to the marital order of human sexuality. When St. Paul defines authority, he goes back to the beginning of creation and teaches that authority is embedded in the very structure of the man/woman relation. Yes, the man is head because, like Christ, he is a cause. The woman is from him and for him (1 Cor 11:8–9) and, as verses 11–12 affirm, the man and woman are defined in relation to each other. Man is from woman. This forms the basis of her authority. But man is not just from woman only in the biological sense that women give birth to males. 1 Corinthians 11:11–12 is the doctrine

---

6. See C.K. Barrett and Earl Muller, S.J. for a fuller discussion of the theological significance of head covering. See footnotes two and eight for references.

7. Earl Muller, S.J., *Trinity and Marriage in Paul: An Establishment of a Communitarian Analogy of the Trinity Grounded in the Theological Shape of Pauline Thought* (New York: Peter Lang, 1990), 302; Barrett, A Commentary, 248–9.

of Genesis: "It is not good that the man should be alone" (Gen 2:18). The creation of the woman is the climax of creation. Eve, though derived from Adam, completes him. She is his body: "bone of my bones and flesh of my flesh." Eve provides Adam with his masculine self-identification. Furthermore, in relation to Adam Eve is also a source: "The man called his wife's name Eve, because she was the mother of all the living" (Gen 3:20).

God observes in Genesis 2:18 that: "It is not good that the man should be alone." The next verse is probably the most misunderstood passage in the Bible: "I will make a suitable partner for him" (NAB). Some passages translate the original ancient Hebrew text as "I will make a helper fit for him," or as we find in the King James version: "I will make a help meet for him." Such translations give the definite impression that the woman is secondary to the man, as if Adam is given primary responsibilities and the woman is there to simply help him—as a person in charge of a project may have an assistant. But the word *helper* of Genesis 2:18 does not mean that the woman is simply man's helper in a functional sense. The noun usually translated "helper" is *ézer*, derived from the verb *ázar*, which means to "save from extremity, to deliver from death." For example, the word would be used to describe the action of giving water to someone dying of thirst, or placing a tourniquet on the arm of someone bleeding to death.[8] If this is so, the word *helper* achieves a whole new dimension. Certainly *ézer* does not describe someone who is inferior or subordinate. Indeed, the *ézer* is a kind of savior figure, and thus the woman is created to rescue man from his original condition of "extremity"— in other words, from isolation, which is the antithesis of authentic human living. The woman exercises a true authority—we may say a true strength—in relation to the man, as she saves him from the "not good" from which the man needed to be freed. Eve brings Adam into

---

8. Samuel Terrien, *Till the Heart Sings* (Philadelphia: Fortress Press, 1985), 10–11.

human communion and thus with her is created the moral center of creation: marriage and the family. Eve is not simply man's "helper"; she is the queen of the created order. She "helps" in the same sense that someone comes to the rescue of another about to die.

The sexual differentiation and dependency of man and woman is the basis of the Christ/Church relation and the order of ecclesial authority. The authority of women in the Church rests on this fact: the Church, in a true sense, is the completion of Christ as Eve is the completion of Adam. The marital order of the man/woman relation taught in 1 Corinthians 11:11–12 is expressed more fully in St. Paul's Letter to the Ephesians. Christ is Head because He is the cause of the Body, the Church. Since the Christ/Church relation is inherently marital, the Church actually completes Christ and is His partner in the salvation of the world. Ephesians 1:22–23 states: "He [God] has put all things under his feet and has made him the head over all things for the Church, which is his body, the fullness of him who fills all in all." Sometimes the word *fullness* (or ***plērōma***) means that the Church is filled with Christ in the sense that she is a passive receptacle into which He has poured His benefits. However, the passive tense of the word *plērōma* at the end of 1:23 can be given an active or passive interpretation. The word *fullness* that precedes the word *fills* or *filling* is rendered in the active sense. The Church completes Christ and is the complement to the Head. Ephesians 5:23 calls the Church Christ's Body in an explicitly marital context. Since the Body completes the Head, the Church is the Lord's complement—she is His fullness! The Christ/Church unity is the ultimate resolution of the "it is not good" of the Beginning, as the *plērōma* of the Church parallels the *ézer* of Eve to Adam. This does not mean that Christ lacks anything according to His divine nature. Colossians 2:9 states that the fullness of the Godhead dwells in Christ bodily. And yet the Church is united to Christ's Godhead and humanity.

At first glance, the Church as the completion of Christ might seem scandalous, as if to imply that Christ lacks something. But the scandal is derived from thinking according to a monist philosophy. We tend to think that if Christ is Lord, He does not need the Church. But reality, even in the Trinity, is not monist; it is communitarian and covenantal. Of course, Christ is perfect. But perfection in the Christian world (as opposed to the pagan) does not mean autonomy, isolation, or radical individualistic self-sufficiency. Salvation is not the result of the isolated Christ but rather of the Mystical Body of Christ. The Church as the fullness of Christ, in the sense of His completion, is affirmed by Pope Pius XII in his encyclical *Mystici Corporis*:

> This communication of the Spirit of Christ is the channel through which all the gifts, powers, and extra-ordinary graces found superabundantly in the Head as in their source flow into all the members of the Church, and are perfected daily in them according to the place they hold in the Mystical Body of Jesus Christ. Thus the Church becomes, as it were, the filling out and the complement of the Redeemer, while Christ in a sense attains through the Church a fullness in all things. . . . Herein we find the reason why, according to the opinion of Augustine . . . the mystical Head, which is Christ, and the Church, which here below as another Christ shows forth His person, constitute one new man, in whom heaven and earth are joined together in perpetuating the saving work of the Cross: Christ We mean, the Head and the Body, the whole Christ.[9]

A distinction exists between Christ and the Church. Christ is not the Body; the Church is the Body. But there is a free relation between them. The key to understanding how the Church is the fullness of Christ is found in Ephesians 5:29. St. Paul teaches that the

---

9. *Mystici Corporis Christi*, no. 77.

Church is Christ's flesh as the body of a wife is the flesh of her husband. The Head gave Himself up for the Body. Now husbands are to:

> . . . love their wives as their own bodies. He who loves his wife loves himself. For no man ever hates his own flesh, but nourishes and cherishes it, as Christ does the Church, because we are members of his body. (Eph 5:28–30)

The woman is the flesh of her spouse and the answer to his solitude. She is his suitable partner, fulfilling what it means for him to be male and to be a head. Thus the Church is the covenantal partner of Christ in redemption. Ephesians 3:10–11 teaches that "through the Church the manifold wisdom of God might now be made known to the principalities and powers in the heavenly places. This was according to the eternal purpose which he has realized in Christ Jesus our Lord." The Church, in union with Christ, reveals God's wisdom. Redemption is not accomplished by Christ alone. It is accomplished by Christ in union with His Church. This is a marriage. Together they make up the "one-flesh" of the New Covenant.

THE FONT AND THE WOMB

In one of his sermons St. Augustine preached: "Your Father is God; the Church is your mother."[10] Many early Church Fathers taught that Christians were brought to life by collaboration between the heavenly Father and His Church. St. Augustine compared man's experience of the Spirit of God to his earthly birth. The former is man's spiritual parturition in which there is "no labor, no misery, no weeping, no death" but only "blessing, joy, and life."[11] Our earthly parents are actually an imperfect sign of the perfect reality that exists in Father

---

10. St. Augustine, *Sermon 216*, 8, trans. Sr. Mary Sarah Muldowny, R.S.N., *Fathers of the Church*, Vol. 38 (New York: Fathers of the Church, Inc., 1959), 157–8 (PL 38.1081).

11. Ibid.

God and Mother Church. They are our true parents. The Father does not beget life alone. God is a Father in union with the Church. Everlasting life is achieved by a birth that involves the parentage of them both. The Church's motherhood is extremely important, which is why the great St. Cyprian, bishop and martyr, could say: "You cannot have God for your Father if you have not the Church for your mother."[12] Because all Christians are born through Mother Church, she is the cause of Christian unity. Christians have a spiritual blood tie by being born from this one mother, and as such the Church's motherhood is the antidote to divisions and schisms. Furthermore, the Church is not simply *another* mother; she is *the* mother of all Christians because, as Origen taught, she is the faithful spouse of Christ: "Through her He begets sons and daughters for Himself."[13]

The fatherhood of God and the motherhood of the Church are realized in the Sacrament of Baptism. The Church Fathers looked upon the baptismal font as the Church's womb. Catechumens experienced a new birth from this womb. From within the house of their Mother they are enabled to pray to the Father.[14] In AD 365, St. Optatus refuted Donatist errors and stated that it is through the "sacramental womb" of the Church that God becomes the Father of men. Baptism is identified as the womb of the Church.[15]

Didymus the Blind (d. AD 398) believed that Baptism fulfilled Psalms 27: "For my father and my mother have forsaken me, but the

---

12. St. Cyprian, *On the Unity of the Church*, 6, trans. Maurice Bevenot, S.J., *Ancient Christian Writers*, Vol. 25 (Westminster, MD: The Newman Press, 1957), 48–9 (CCL 3.253).

13. Origen, *Exp. in Prov.* in Joseph C. Plumpe, *Mater Ecclesia: An Inquiry Into the Concept of Church as Mother in Early Christianity* (Wash., D.C.: The Catholic University of America Press, 1943), 78 (PG 17.201,202).

14. Tertullian, *On Baptism*, 20, *The Ante-Nicene Fathers*, Vol. 3, eds. Alexander Roberts and James Donaldson (Grand Rapids, MI: Wm. B. Eerdmans, 1957), 679 (CSEL 20.218).

15. St. Optatus, *Contra Parmenianum Donatistam*, 4, 2 in Walter M. Bedard, *The Symbolism of the Baptismal Font in Early Christian Thought* (Wash., D.C.: The Catholic University of America Press, 1951), 2 & 26 (CSEL 26.103).

Lord will take me up" (verse 10). Our first parents were Adam and Eve, who by sin lost for man the gift of life. But the Christian receives new parents in Baptism, where he is given the Church for a mother, for Father the Most High God, and for brother Christ Himself.[16]

The holy partnership of regeneration is very strongly expressed by St. Augustine. The Christian obtains God for a Father when he is conceived by the seed of God in the baptismal font that Augustine calls "the womb of the Church."[17] Elsewhere, Augustine even refers to the font by the more graphic and less poetic term "uterus."[18] St. Augustine speaks of the life-giving powers of the Church very explicitly when he cautions catechumens not to receive Baptism until they are ready:

> O you who are being born [to the faith], whom the Lord has made, strive to be born in sound and healthful fashion, lest you be prematurely and disastrously delivered. Behold the womb of your mother, the Church; behold how she labors in pain to bear you and to bring you forth into the light of faith. Do not by your impatience, disturb your mother's body and make narrow the passage of your mother's delivery.[19]

The womb of the Church brings life to men. St. Clement of Alexandria (d. AD 215) teaches, "For this was what was said, 'Unless you be converted, and become as children,' pure in flesh, holy in soul by abstinence from evil deeds; showing that he would have us be such as also He generated us from our mother, the water."[20] The rebirth of the Christian is through the baptismal womb of the Church, and

---

16. Didymus of Alexandria, *De Trinitate*, 2, 13, Bedard, 21 (PG 39.691–692).

17. St. Augustine, *Sermon 56*, 5, Bedard, 29 (PL 38.379).

18. St. Augustine, *Sermon 119*, 4, *A Library of the Fathers of the Holy Catholic Church*, Vol. 16 (Oxford: John Henry Parker, 1844, 506 (PL 38.674).

19. St. Augustine, *Sermon 216*, 7, p. 156 (PL 38.1080).

20. St. Clememt of Alexandria, *The Stromata*, 4, 25, *The Ante-Nicene Fathers*, Vol. 2, eds. Alexander Roberts and James Donaldson (Grand Rapids, MI: Wm. B. Eerdmans, 1962), 439 (PG 8.1370).

again St. Clement shows that this birth is through the union of Father God and Mother Church. He has begotten us through her. St. Ephrem, a fourth century Eastern writer, equates Baptism with the womb of the Church in which children are conceived bearing the image of Christ. In Baptism they come out of the water pure children who went down into the water with defilements. Baptism is "another womb" that has the power to make young people out of old.[21] St. Methodius, in his work *The Banquet of the Ten Virgins*, also teaches that in baptismal rebirth the Christian takes on the image of Christ. Concerning the Woman of the Apocalypse, the character Thecla says that it is Mother Church who brings about this marvelous rebirth of human beings. This rebirth is indeed the Church's unique and definitive task.

A partnership of regeneration exists between the Holy Spirit and the baptismal womb of the Church. Theodore of Mopsuestia states that the bishop is the mediator of the Spirit in Baptism. Through his action, standing on the side of God the Father, the bishop makes the water capable of begetting new life. In this way Nicodemus' question is answered: "Can [a man] enter a second time into his mother's womb and be born?" (Jn 3:4). Jesus replied that one is born of the water and the Spirit. In natural birth the mother's womb receives a seed that is formed by the hand of God. Likewise in Baptism "the water becomes a womb to receive the person who is being born, but it is the grace of the Spirit which forms him there for a second birth and makes him a completely new man."[22] In Baptism the one to be reborn "settles in the water as in a kind of womb."[23] This imagery is reminiscent of how the newly conceived human zygote will implant himself/herself into the lush crimson lining of the mother's womb

21. St. Ephrem, Hymni de virgininate, 7, 5, Bedard, 19.

22. St. Theodore of Mopsuestia, *Baptismal Homily III* in Edward Yarnold, S.J., The Awe Inspiring Rites if Initiation; *Baptismal Homilies of the Fourth Century* (Slough, England: St. Paul Publications, 1971), 194–5.

23. Ibid.

and be nourished there in preparation for birth. But in Baptism it is Mother Church to whom we must be attached.

BAPTISM AND MARY

St. Ambrose, the fourth century bishop of Milan, sees a parallel between Mary's conception of Christ by the Holy Spirit and the regeneration of the Christian in Baptism.

> For Mary did not conceive of man, but received of the Holy Spirit in her womb. . . . If, then, the Holy Spirit coming upon the Virgin effected conception, and effected the work of generation, surely there must be no doubt that the Spirit, coming upon the Font, or upon those who obtain baptism, effects the truth of regeneration.[24]

Mary conceived the Son of God by the power of the Holy Spirit. This same Spirit is invoked by the minister of Baptism over the waters of the font, which is the Church's sacramental womb. The Church's life-giving powers, and thus the center of her authority, exist according to the pattern of Mary's own maternity and covenant partnership with God. This is why the Church's motherhood is not mere sentimentality. Motherhood expresses a reality about the Church. The great twentieth century theologian Henri de Lubac, quoting the great Mathias Scheeben, states:

> "The motherhood of the Church," wrote Scheeben, "is not an empty title, it is not a weak analogy of natural motherhood. It does not signify only that the Church acts like a tender mother towards us. . . . This motherhood is as real

---

24. St. Ambrose, *The Mysteries*, 9, 59, *Fathers of the Church*, Vol. 44 (Wash. D.C.: Catholic University of America Press, 1963), 28 (CSEL 73.115–116).

as the presence of Christ in the Eucharist, or as real as the supernatural life that exists in the children of God."[25]

If the motherhood of the Church is as real as the presence of Christ in the Eucharist, it is because as a mother she carries on the truth about a person: the New Eve, Mary, mother of all the living.

The ancient liturgy of the Mozarabic Rite of the Spanish Church announces clearly that the maternal powers of the Church first existed in the Mother of God:

> The one gave salvation to the nations, the other gives the nations to the Savior. The one carried life in her womb, the other carries it in the sacramental font. What was once accorded to Mary in the carnal order is now accorded spiritually to the Church. She conceives the Word in her unfailing faith, she gives birth to it in a spirit freed from all corruption, she holds it in a soul covered with the Virtue of the Most High.[26]

THE CHURCH WHO GIVES BIRTH

The Church continues Mary's life-giving activity. St. Augustine once wrote: "If she [the Church] gives birth to the members of Christ, then she is absolutely the same as Mary."[27] This means that the Church possesses a life-giving authority patterned on Mary. It is a life-giving authority that is actually a vital part of salvation in Christ. His redemption is accomplished within the maternal Marian power of the Church to produce His members—those who are saved in Him. God

25. Henri de Lubac, *Motherhood of the Church* (San Francisco: Ignatius Press, 1982), 39.

26. Ibid., p. 58.

27. St. Augustine, *Sermon Morin*, 1, 1, *St. Augustine: Le Visage de L'Élgise*, ed. Hans Urs Von Balthasar, *Unam Sanctam 31* (Paris: Éditions du Cerf, 1958), 187.

was not made man without the cooperation of a woman. Thus man cannot be saved apart from the maternal activity of the Church.

St. Paul spoke about the motherhood of the Church in his Letter to the Galatians. Here the Apostle contrasts the Old and the New Covenant. Christians are "children of the promise" (Gal 4:28) because they are born of the New Jerusalem—born "of a free woman" (Gal 4:31). For St. Paul, Hagar and Sarah are symbolically prophetic. Hagar is unfree, a slave girl who stands for the covenant of Mt. Sinai and brings forth children unto slavery. Sarah is free, a free woman who stands for the Church of our time and brings forth children who will inherit the promises of God. A woman is the sign of the Church, and this is specifically realized in her procreative life-giving powers. Sarah, furthermore, was barren, but God had made her fruitful (Gal 4:27).

The Pauline teaching on the two women and the two covenants is important for a number of reasons. First, as we have already noted, it is women who stand for the covenants, especially in their ability to bear children. Secondly, one must be born of this second mother to inherit these promises. St. Paul does not say that the New Covenant is *like* a mother; he says she *is* our mother. The terminology in verse 26 is personal and real. It calls up sentiments of devotion, affection, and gratitude. The Christian should not be indifferent to the fact that the New Covenant is the mother to whom he owes his life. It is God who has made Sarah fruitful, and likewise, the Church is made fruitful through her covenant relation with God. Finally, St. Paul implies that God has become the husband of this fruitful Church when he quotes Isaiah: "Rejoice, O barren one who does not bear; break forth and shout, you who are not with labor pains; for the desolate has more children than she who has a husband" (Gal 4:27). St. Paul quotes from Isaiah 54:1. Only a few verses later, this same Old Testament prophet specifically states that God is the husband of this barren women: "For you will forget the shame of your youth, and the reproach of your widowhood you will remember no more. For your Maker is your husband, the Lord of hosts is his name" (Is 54:4–5).

Christians become the children of the New Covenant with God as their Father because they are born of the New Jerusalem. St. Cyril of Jerusalem used St. Paul's teaching from Galatians 4:21–31 in direct reference to the Catholic Church. In an address to catechumens he states:

> . . . the Catholic Church. For this is the peculiar name of this Holy Church, the mother of us all, which is the spouse of Our Lord Jesus Christ . . . and is a figure and a copy of the Jerusalem which is above, which is free, and the mother of us all; which before was barren, but now has many children.[28]

The Jerusalem above that St. Paul spoke about is also found in Revelation 21. She is the New Jerusalem "coming down out of heaven from God, prepared as a bride adorned for her husband" (21:2). The wedding between Christ and the Church fulfills the covenant of redemption: "Behold, the dwelling of God is with men. He will dwell with them, and they shall be his people, and God himself will be with them" (21:3).

THE CHURCH WHO FEEDS HER CHILDREN

Priests, acting *in persona Christi*, are the official dispensers of the sacraments, but the sacraments can only be dispensed through Mother Church. St. Hippolytus teaches that Eve has become the Church. God has

---

28. St. Cyril of Jerusalem, *Catechesis XVIII*, 26, *The Nicene and Post-Nicene Fathers*, Vol. 7, eds. Philip Schaff and Henry Wace (Grand Rapids, MI: Wm. B. Eerdmans, 1955), 140.

raised Eve who is not seduced. . . . O blessed woman who does not desire to be apart from Christ. Accept this Eve, she who does not engender us in sorrow. Accept the New Eve, the Living One upon whom one can rely. . . . After her union with the Incorruptible One she wishes to provide nourishment by which human nature will no longer have to hunger and thirst. Henceforth Eve is a true companion for Adam. O what admirable aid—she brings Him to us by the proclamation of the Gospel. . . . Her children drink from the milk of her breast, each one drinks from the law of the Gospel, harvesting food for eternity.[29]

The Church as Christ's companion is the mediatrix of life, a nurturing mother. The Church feeds her children by the Gospel preached within her. Where the Church is, there is the Spirit. A person partakes of the Spirit when he is nourished from the mother's breasts; otherwise, a person is drinking polluted water from broken vessels.[30] The Church as a mother possesses authority because access to God is achieved through her. The Church is the repository of faith. A person has life when he is connected to her and allows himself to be fed on her doctrine that has been entrusted to her by God.

The Virgin Mother Church feeds her children with holy milk. St. Paul said, "I fed you with milk, not solid food; for you were not ready for it" (1 Cor 3:2). St. Clement taught that this milk was Christ the Word that came down like manna in the form of the preached Gospel.[31] St. Cyprian also spoke of the Church as a mother who feeds her children through the milk of her breasts:

---

29. St. Hippolytus, *Commentary on the Canticle*, Fragm., slav. XV, in Karl Delahaye, *Ecclesia Mater chez les Pères des Trois Premiers Siècles, Unam Sanctam* 46 (Paris: Éditions du Cerf, 1964), 93–4.

30. Ibid., 94.

31. Plumpe, *Mater Ecclesia*, 65.

[The Church] spreads her branches in generous growth over all the earth, she extends her abundant streams even further; yet one is the headspring, one the source, one the mother who is prolific in her offspring, generation after generation; of her womb we are born, of her milk we are fed, of her Spirit our souls draw their life-breath [32]

St. Cyprian's words are very powerful in their simplicity. He teaches very distinctly that Mother Church is a source in the sense of being an origin of life. In this way her maternal authority flows as from a "headspring." Later in the same passage, Cyprian warns that one must remain connected to Mater Ecclesia: "You cannot have God for your Father if you have not the Church as your Mother."[33] When a person withdraws from the Church he perishes. St. Augustine also supports St. Cyprian's teaching. No one can have God for Father if he despises the Church, his mother. The Christian must love the Church and stay attached to her because she provides spiritual nourishment, giving her children bread from heaven, the Holy Eucharist. For this reason Mother Church should never be abandoned.[34]

Christ feeds His people through the priesthood, but Christians are fed by Christ on the Eucharist and the other sacraments according to the same salvific order by which Christ became man. The Church, like Mary, is an historical entity called by God to be a vehicle of His grace. God became man through a woman. Mary gave the Second Person of the Trinity His historical real presence, and thus the people of God receive the Body of Christ from the Church that lives according to the Marian maternal principle. As Mary gave us Christ, the Church gives us Christ.

The spiritual nourishment the Church provides to the faithful within the sacramental system is intrinsic to the motherhood of the

---

32. St. Cyprian, *Unity*, 5, p. 48.
33. Ibid., 48–9.
34. St. Augustine, Sermon Mai 92, *Le Visage*, 172–3.

Church. It is part of the feminine responsibility for the faith. Sexual symbolism as an expression of the Church's maternity is very important. The Church's motherhood is not a mere poetic metaphor; the Church who nourishes the faithful provides her children with a food that is her own. Grace and the Holy Spirit are as intrinsic to the Church as milk is to a nursing mother. The Lord is within the Church as He dwelt in the womb of the Virgin. We are fed by what comes through the Church and what is of the Body of Christ. A male, unlike a female, has no food within him by which others may be fed. A man feeds others by foreign substances he acquires from outside of himself. This is not so for the pregnant mother or the new birth mother. We should be careful, however, not to fall into the error of saying that the Church is the source of the sacraments herself. We must avoid turning the Church into a humanist project. The sacraments are obtainable through the Church within the covenantal union that exists between her and Christ. St. Augustine spoke so beautifully of this union whereby the Church becomes the font of the sacraments. The Church has her being from the side of the slain Christ, from whose side "the sacraments flowed forth." In this water and blood the New Eve is created.[35]

A parallel exists between Adam and Eve, and Christ and the Church. As our physical nature came from Adam through Eve, so our spiritual life comes from Christ through the Church. She is our Second Mother.[36] The living waters that come from the side of Christ flow through her into the world, making her a fertile mother.

The Christian actually never outgrows the Mater Ecclesia. The entire patristic witness declares that those who do leave her risk eternal damnation. St. Cyprian teaches: "She it is that keeps us unharmed for God, she appoints the sons she has begotten to His

35. St. Augustine, *Psalm 41*, *Nicene and Post-Nicene Fathers*, Vol. 3, 222 (PL 37.1672)

36. Plumpe, *Mater Ecclesia*, 57.

kingdom."[37] Salvation is dependent on remaining inside the womb of the Body, Mother Church, wherein the Christian is nourished on the food of God.

MATER ET MAGISTRA

Because the Church gives birth to God's children, she has been entrusted with the godly education of these children. The instructive task of the Magisterium is accomplished within the Church as mother. She too is a teacher. She guides, directs, protects, and educates the faithful unto eternal life through the Word and the sacraments. Priests as fathers feed the flock under their care, but the whole Church as mother is entrusted with the spiritual upbringing of her children. Tertullian taught that the Church was not only a mother by Baptism, but also through the education of her children afterwards. The Christian who fell into heresy was motherless.[38] St. Hippolytus connects the preaching task of the Church to her maternal power: "The church will not cease to bear from her heart . . . the Word . . . by which is meant that the church, always bringing forth Christ, . . . becomes the instructor of all nations."[39] St. Pope John XXIII confirmed that the Church is both mother and teacher in his famous encyclical *Mater et Magistra*.

> Mother and Teacher of all nations—such is the Catholic Church in the mind of her Founder, Jesus Christ; to hold the world in an embrace of love, that men, in every age, should find in her their own completeness in a higher order of living, and their ultimate salvation. She is "the pillar and ground of the truth." To her was entrusted by her holy

---

37. St. Cyprian, *Unity*, 6, p. 48.

38. Tertullian, *De praescriptione haereticorum*, 42, (CSEL 70.55).

39. St. Hippolytus, *The Anti-Christ*, 61, *The Ante-Nicene Fathers*, Vol. 5, eds. Alexander Roberts and James Donaldson (Grand Rapids, MI: Wm. B. Eerdmans, 1957), 217 (PG 10.779–782).

Founder the twofold task of giving life to her children and of teaching them and guiding them—both as individuals and as nations—with maternal care.[40]

The Acts of the Apostles 1:12–14 records that Mary was present in the midst of the Eleven in the Upper Room. As she stood at the foot of the Cross, Christ appointed Mary the mother of John and she became "the mother of all living." Certainly Mary transmitted to John and to the primitive Church all her knowledge of Christ. What she pondered in her heart (Lk 2:19, 51) has become the treasure of the Church that exists in her image. According to the model of the Blessed Virgin, the Church teaches by revealing the mystery of her Son. This is the fundamental educative task with which she has been entrusted by God. The Church educates not only by gentle guidance, who submissively receives whatever comes from the bishop's hand, but at times she must educate by fighting for the proper food for her children—the food that her Lord and Spouse wills that she have, and of which, by right, she refuses to be deprived. The Church as Mother contains in herself an authority to admonish bishops to be true and faithful fathers. Mother Church, often through the voice of the laity, calls them to fulfill their fatherhood. She is their teacher in this sense.

The bosom of Mother Church is a school of divine life. When one enters the Church one is taken into her life, is fed upon her breasts. By her intimate care the Christian is taken into the practice of the faith. Henri de Lubac declared upon his conversion: "Praised be this great majestic Mother, at whose knees I have learned everything!"[41]

---

40. Pope John XXIII, Encyclical Letter On Christianity and Social Progress *Mater et Magistra* (May 15, 1961), no. 1.

41. Paul Claudel as quoted by De Lubac in *Motherhood*, 61.

WOMEN AND THE EUCHARIST

Christ's death on the Cross is the supreme act of the Head. By this sacrifice Christ is the source of the Body. The Church is the Bride of Christ, the flesh that completes Him. The one flesh of Christ and the Church is made real in the world through the celebration of the Holy Eucharist. The Mass is not a monist re-presentation of Christ. True worship is brought about through the union of Christ and His people. Christ's redemptive role is an inherently masculine one. The Church's redemptive role, in relation to Him, is no less inherently feminine. The Christian woman then possesses authority to be the full sign of the covenantal response of the Church to Christ. The Christian woman is the Church's symbol of her response that completes and fulfills the covenant by which the world is saved.

We can see the Eucharistic contribution of women when we look at Mary. During Christ's sacrifice on the Cross, Mary, the Church's prototype, stood nearby. As Christ's mother, Mary suffered with her Son, lifting up herself with Him and associating "herself with a maternal heart with His sacrifice" (*Lumen Gentium*, 58). By making present the sacrifice of Christ, the Eucharist also causes the sacrifice of Mary to be present, who on Calvary made the response of the Church.[42]

When Mary said yes to the angel, her response stood for all mankind. Woman confirms the goodness of creation. The freedom of man is manifested in Mary as she stands in for liberated mankind precisely as a woman.[43] Creation, coming from God's hand, restored by grace, can give its own response in love back to God. In the Eucharist, Christ comes down to us, but it is not only that. The Eucharist is the response of the Bride, her sacrifice of praise and

---

42. John Paul II, "At the Root of the Eucharist is the Virginal Heart of Mary," *L'Osservatore Romano* (June 13, 1983), 2.

43. Joseph Cardinal Ratzinger, "On the Position of Mariology and Marian Spirituality Within the Totality of Faith" in *The Church and Women*, ed. Helmut Moll (San Francisco: Ignatius Press, 1988), 76.

thanksgiving, in that joyous one-flesh union that is ours. Vatican II teaches: "Christ indeed always associates the Church with Himself in this great work wherein God is perfectly glorified and men are sanctified. The Church is His beloved Bride who calls to her Lord, and through Him offers worship to the Eternal Father."[44] The one-flesh, nuptial meaning of creation protects the Church against a dry and stunted Christomonism.

In the Eucharist it is the woman, as the locus of everything good about creation, who provides the necessary sacramental response by which the "one-flesh" unity of Christ and the Church is expressed in history. Without the feminine response to God, Christian worship would be meaningless. In fact, Christianity would be some other kind of religion; if the symbols of human sexuality by which the Church worships are altered, the religion itself collapses.

If the ministerial priesthood is rooted in the meaning of male authority, then certainly it is true that the sacrifice of praise offered by the common priesthood in the Eucharist has a distinctly feminine character. Of course, this common priesthood of the faithful is exercised by men as well as women, but women as symbols of Christ's Bride exemplify these sacrifices. The Church's sacrifice of praise finds its truest meaning liturgically expressed through female sexuality. The Eucharist is offered by the whole Christ—the *Christus totus*. Many who favor women's ordination think that the male priest acting *in persona Christi* is a sure sign that the Mass is male dominated and male centered. In the feminist mind the sanctuary is the domain of power; however, men do not dominate the liturgy. It is permeated by femininity, by the totally indispensable role women play in the Church's worship. The Mass is the celebration of the Beloved's love for the Bride, and woman is the concrete, historical sign of this Bride. Indeed, the priestly office exists to serve, not itself, but the life-giving power of the Church, who is at once a glorious wife

---

44. *Sacrosanctum Concilium*, no. 7.

and mother in the pattern of Mary, the ecclesial Madonna whose song is praise.

7

MOTHERS OF THE CHURCH

At the age of thirty-six I suppose one could say that I married rather late in life. I was still attending college in the midst of completing my doctorate at Marquette University in Milwaukee—when Edmund and I became husband and wife. While researching and composing my dissertation, I taught theology courses to undergraduates at the Jesuit-run school. Though I was the instructor and had a certain measure of academic authority, in some ways I still thought of myself as a member of the student body, a class of persons without the usual responsibilities of life and in a stage of transition. Even marriage didn't really make me feel any different, and conceiving a child and sadly experiencing a miscarriage didn't make me feel any different either. I still identified with that young, untested class of persons called college students even though I was pushing forty!

Then I became pregnant for the second time. By the fifth month or so it became obvious that I was expecting, and it became very obvious to my students as well. I remember very distinctly one day donning a maternity dress and standing in front of my Christian Anthropology class when a certain odd sensation came over me. I suddenly felt like a full-fledged adult. I was now, because of this pregnancy, somehow separated from the students I was teaching. I was no longer one of them. I was truly their teacher. I had a responsibility and authority that they didn't have. I felt I was truly different from them and had crossed over to adulthood.

I have pondered the meaning of being swept by that strange realization. Certainly before marriage and pregnancy I had attended to adult responsibilities, even engaging in acts of civil disobedience, standing trial, and spending time in jail for the pro-life cause. Yet it was carrying a child that made me feel like I was now truly an adult. Undoubtedly it had something to do with the fact that giving life to another was not only obvious to me, but publicly obvious to others that marked me off. Now even the world outside of my own little world expected something from me; they knew I had to extend myself to another, and that society took for granted this expectation that I would fulfill. I was no longer just part of a college student culture and identity. With the pregnancy I took on a new cultural, societal status that comes from the uniquely feminine responsibility of caring for new life that is absolutely helpless and dependent. I had been entrusted with the life of another and thus my role as an expectant mother was a symbol of a profound feminine power—dare I use that word—that even commanded a certain awe, reverence, and respect. The pregnant woman is a public teacher with a peculiarly feminine lesson that it is indeed the woman who is the center of communal ties and human relatedness. The woman can best transmit spiritual and moral values to others because of her unique powers of receptivity. Furthermore, female sexuality is the primary symbol of human receptivity to the offer of God's grace in the world.

It should be clear by now that if authority has to do with the power to give life and the responsibilities for life, authority cannot be reduced to mere juridicism. Authority is based in the fundamental mystery of sexuality between men and women, where within the relation between the sexes, creation itself finds its meaning and its order. If the male/female relation is tampered with in any way, the world itself is undone.

The topic of feminine authority produces an anxiousness in people. Some may finally ask impatiently and crudely: "Well, so who do women get to boss around?" Such a question still sees authority as power to control, as a force that is above and outside of a free covenantal relation. If a woman has the right to "boss someone around," this ought only to be done within her realm of responsibility that flows from the female ability to bestow life. A man's authority is not greater than hers and in some important ways it is less. The right to make demands and order others to do things is only authentic authority if its serves life. But a full understanding of women's authority means moving from an abstract discussion to concrete example. Yes, the Church is Bride and Mother who has the authority to complete Christ who is her Head. But how is this authority actually exercised in the particular? How is this authority manifested in the lives of Christian women? How do women take up their own specific responsibility for the faith that stands in relation to male authority in the Church? In the covenant between Christ and the Church, women make real in the world the responsibility for the faith that God has entrusted to the Church, the Bride of Christ. Women, for example, have a nuptial authority to require of their spouses that they exercise their role as husband in the pattern of Christ's love. This is one very strong example of feminine authority. But before we look at women in the Christian dispensation, the Old Testament provides some excellent examples of how women exercised authority.

JUDITH

Judith, a holy and pious widow, became the source of encouragement and hope for the entire Hebrew nation. By her courage and confidence in the face of the Assyrians she reinvigorated the Hebrew nation, in particular the army, rulers, and military leaders. Judith's piety is directly related to her vocation of widowhood in which she lived a life of intense prayer, penance, and fasting (Jud 8:4–8). She held no formal office either by election or by ritual consecration, yet due to her piety she emerged as the teacher of the nation. Judith harshly reprimanded the leaders for their cowardice and gave them spiritual guidance. She told them that they should never have made a deal with God in which they said that they would surrender to the Assyrians in five days unless God provided the Jews with water.

By the power of Judith's prayers she becomes an intercessor between God and the Hebrew people (Jud 9). When she prepares to meet the Assyrians, Judith takes on the appearance of a woman adorned as a bride: "She removed the sackcloth which she had been wearing, and took off her widow's garments . . . and arrayed herself in her most festive apparel, which she used to wear while her husband Manasseh was living" (10:3). St. Ambrose saw in this the image of one who has become Christ's bride. Now she will please, not her dead husband, but a Man who has priority over her husband.[1] Ambrose clearly states that widows are signs of the Church. The widow of Sarepta and the prophet Elijah are an example of this, as their story speaks of the mystery of Christ and the Church.[2] The widow's moral courage is shown by the fact that, although forsaken, she keeps her chastity, which is a sign of enduring faith even in adversity. At various times the Church is "a virgin, married, and a widow." Ambrose teaches that all women who occupy these various states of life "have an example to imitate," namely the Church who possesses these feminine realities in relation to Christ.[3]

The widow's chastity is part of Judith's moral superiority over Holefernes and his men. Her victory over Holefernes is linked to her ability to maintain chastity. Judith's chastity has nuptial significance: "And she did well in resuming her bridal ornaments when about to fight, for the reminders of wedlock are the arms of chastity, and in no other way could a widow please or gain the victory."[4] St. Ambrose

---

1. St. Ambrose, *Liber De Viduis* 7.38 (PL 16.259).
2. Ibid., 3.14 (PL 16.252).
3. Ibid., 3.15.
4. Ibid., 3.16 (PL 16.252–253).

sees chastity as the living expression of an enduring faith in a time when one experiences spiritual desolation. Judith is personally this sign. Indeed, she is the historical reality of Israel's fidelity. By faith she is able to conquer Holefernes. St. Ambrose contributes Judith's victory to her sobriety and temperance, which were precisely the virtues Holefernes and his men lacked. Judith's virtue is the source of male bravery: "And so the temperance, and sobriety of one widow not only subdued her own nature, but, which is far more, even made men more brave."[5] In this Judith exercises true moral leadership that is the basis for a political authority.

DEBORAH

As a judge of Israel, Deborah served as a mother to her people (Judg 5:7). In her favor St. Ambrose states, "A widow, she governs the people. A widow, she chooses generals. A widow, she determines wars and orders triumphs."[6] Ambrose says something one would not expect of a Church Father: that weakness cannot be attributed to sex.[7] Deborah provides wisdom and military leadership by which the Jews overcome Jabin, the Canaanite king who oppressed them for twenty years. St. Ambrose interprets Scripture to mean that Barak is Deborah's son. But the mother is the son's teacher (4:6–7). Barak is completely dependent on her, to the point of refusing to enter battle unless she comes with him (4:8). St. Ambrose comments:

> [T]his widow, before all others, made all the preparations for war. And to show that the needs of the household were not dependent on the public resources, but rather that public duties were guided by the discipline of homelife, she brings

---

5. Ibid.

6. St. Ambrose, *Concerning Widows*, 7, 38, trans. H. De Romestin, *The Nicene and Post-Nicene Fathers*, Vol. 10, ed. Philip Schaff (Grand Rapids, MI: Wm. B. Eerdmans, 1955), 398 (PL 16.259).

7. Ibid., 8,44, p. 399 (PL 16.261).

forth from her home her son as leader of the army, that we may acknowledge that a widow can train a warrior; whom as a mother she taught, as a judge, placed in command, as, being herself brave, she trained him, and as a prophetess sent to certain victory.

And lastly, her son Barak shows the chief part of the victory was in the hands of a woman when he said: "If thou wilt not go with me I will not go, for I know not the day on which the Lord sendeth his angel with me." How great then was the might of that woman to whom the leader of the army says, "If thou wilt not go I will not go."[8]

The phrase "public duties were guided by the discipline of homelife" describes the nature of feminine authority exercised by Deborah. Her public authority is not separate from her domestic authority, but indeed flows from it and derives its authenticity from it.

Deborah leads her son to his destiny and fulfillment and mission for Israel: "How great, I say, the fortitude of the widow who keeps not back her son from dangers through motherly affection, but rather with the zeal of a mother exhorts her son to go forth to victory while saying that the decisive point of that victory is in the hand of a woman."[9] Deborah prefigures Mary, who at Cana directed Christ to the Cross, to the attainment of His victory and the fulfillment of His glory. The "decisive victory is in the hand of a woman" is Deborah's own affirmation that not her son but a woman will actually attain the final triumph: "for the Lord will sell Sisera into the hand of a woman" (Judg 4:9). This woman is Jael. Sisera flees to her tent hoping to gain refuge from Barak's assault. Jael allows him to think that he will have safe refuge with her, but she drives a tent peg through his temple while he sleeps and kills him. Her action is similar to Judith's, who,

8. Ibid.
9. Ibid., 8, 45, 46, p. 399 (PL 16.261–262).

in a tent, cut off Holefernes' head while he was, unconscious, "overcome with wine" (Jud 13:2).

Jael is not a Jew but a member of the Gentile people. St. Ambrose sees in her a type of the Church as the Church rose up from among the Gentiles.[10] Sisera's defeat is an allegory that foretells the Church's victory among the Gentiles. Barak represents the Hebrew people who were the first to put the devil to flight, but because they did not accept Christ, the Jews would not finish the victory. Thus Ambrose concludes: "The commencement of the victory was from the Fathers, its conclusion is in the Church" of which Jael, the Gentile woman, is the prototype.[11] Deborah's authority is a sign of the Church:

> And so according to this history a woman, that the minds of women might be stirred up, became a judge, a woman set all in order, a woman prophesied, a woman triumphed, and joining in the battle array taught men to war under a woman's lead. But in a mystery it is the battle of faith and the victory of the Church.[12]

There can be no doubt that this Church Father recognizes that a woman can hold considerable authority! She puts all in order and even teaches men how to wage war. But this authority has a transcendent value. It is the concrete manifestation, even in an Old Testament figure, of the authority of the feminine Church.

STS. PERPETUA AND FELICITY

One of the most compelling stories of early Christian martyrdom is the passion of Sts. Perpetua and Felicity during the reign of Septimus Severus in AD 202. One is immediately struck by the man-

---

10. Ibid., 8, 46 (PL 16.262).
11. Ibid., 8, 47.
12. Ibid., 8, 48.

ner in which these women exercised their motherhood toward their own children while suffering the deprivations of prison life. Literally mothers in the flesh, they kept the faith during persecution and thus are mothers of the Church as well.

The narrator of their martyrdom describes Perpetua as a young twenty-two-year-old "with an infant son at the breast."[13] She dutifully nurses her son while imprisoned and must suffer the constant pleadings of her father to renounce the Christian faith and gain her freedom. The aged father's persistent argument is that Perpetua should do this for the sake of the family. Although Perpetua is the one living in a dungeon, she comforts and supplies encouragement to her family when she, of course, is in need of such things from them. As long as Perpetua has her child with her she considers the dungeon her true home: "Forthwith I grew strong, and was relieved from distress and anxiety about my infant; and the dungeon became to me as it were a palace, so that I preferred being there to being elsewhere."

Perpetua's fidelity to the faith makes her the superior of her father. Once again he tries to persuade her to give up the Christian faith. He is her chief tempter. His attempts to persuade her are even described by Perpetua as his "seeking to turn me away and cast me down from the faith." For her to be "cast down" would place her on the same level as her father. Even the father recognizes that Perpetua's fidelity to Christ has caused a dramatic shift in their relationship. He must appeal to her no longer as "daughter," which was his chief weapon against her, but now acknowledges her as "lady." The father cannot manipulate the affections of his daughter, but must appeal to her as a woman with authority to say yes or no. Ironically, her refusal to deny Christ causes her father to suffer the persecution that Christians endure. While trying to cast down Perpetua from the faith, he is seized at the prison by Hilarianus, the procurator, and beaten with rods.

---

13. Ibid, 8, 50 (PL 16.263).

St. Felicity is in prison while eight months pregnant, and she gives birth in the dungeon to a baby daughter. In giving birth to this child she gives birth to her own martyrdom. As long as she remained pregnant her life was spared, for "pregnant women are not allowed to be publicly punished." She longed to give birth so that she might join the martyrdom of her fellow prisoners. Her martyrdom is specifically understood in terms of a second birth: "Felicity was there, rejoicing that she had safely given birth so that she might fight with the wild beasts, from the blood of the midwife to the blood of the gladiator, to wash after childbirth with a second baptism."[14] Not only is Felicity's martyrdom a chance for her to give birth a second time, but note that both births are understood in terms of struggle and combat—contests with blood. Her martyrdom is taken on as a feminine power to undergo travail and give life.

How interesting that it is precisely the feminine nature that Perpetua and Felicity's captors ridicule. Stripped naked and placed on exhibition before the people, they are threatened with death by a "very fierce cow" the devil has prepared for them, "mocking their sex in that of the beasts." Felicity faces this beast "with breasts still dripping from her recent childbirth." There is not a more compelling image of female martyrdom in all Christian writing. Earlier, Perpetua had a vision in which she was stripped "and became a man," wherein her spiritual battle of martyrdom in the arena takes on the character of a gladiatorial contest. But when actual martyrdom occurs, any sense of a masculine battle disappears. Instead, Perpetua is fully a woman, no longer a strong gladiator rubbed with oil. She comes before her torturers a "woman of delicate frame," while Felicity's breasts are weighted with the milk of her motherhood.

Perpetua's vision of herself as a gladiator seems to be fulfilled at the end of the passion narrative. Indeed, she does do battle with a

---

14. "The Passion of Sts. Perpetua and Felicity" in *The Living Testament: The Essential Writings of Christianity Since the Bible*, ed. M Basil Pennington, et al. (San Francisco: Harper and Row Publishers, 1985), 34.

young gladiator who is actually afraid to kill her because of her purity and womanly authority:

> Perpetua, that she might taste some pain being pierced between the ribs, cried out loudly, and she herself placed the wavering hand of the youthful gladiator to her throat. Possibly such a woman could not have been slain unless she herself had willed it, because she was feared by the impure spirit.[15]

The captors are not in control of the women. The women are in control of them. Furthermore, the women serve as the spiritual leaders of other Christians, both men and women, who are also awaiting martyrdom. Just prior to her own death, Perpetua encourages the others and is their spiritual teacher: "Stand fast in the faith, and love one another, all of you, and be not offended at my sufferings."

The passion of Sts. Perpetua and Felicity has stood in Christian tradition as a paradigm of feminine courage through which the faith of the Church has been fostered.

THE MOTHERHOOD OF BLANDINA

The martyrdom of Blandina and her companions under Marcus Aurelius in AD 177 is recorded by Eusebius in his *Ecclesiastical History*.[16] Again we are presented with a woman of rare courage who is the chief spiritual leader of the martyrs of Vienne and Lyon. Eusebius describes her many tortures and her remarkable ability, despite a weak body, to endure it all. One of her tortures was to be hung on a cross:

> By her firmly intoned prayer, she inspired the combatants with great zeal, as they looked on during the contest and

---

15. Ibid., 35.

16. My commentary is based upon "The Passion of Sts. Perpetua and Felicity" cited in footnote 14.

with their outward eyes saw through their sister Him who was crucified for them, that He might persuade those who believe in Him that everyone who suffers for the glory of Christ always has fellowship with the living God.[17]

Blandina takes on the role of mother to the other Christian captives. She took Ponticus, a fifteen-year-old boy, under her care and gave him the necessary strength of spirit to undergo torture for the faith: "For Ponticus was encouraged by his sister, so that even the heathen saw that she was urging him on and encouraging him, and after he had nobly endured every torture he gave up the ghost."

Blandina saw to it that not one of her children perished, in the sense that all of the imprisoned Christians maintained their faith in Christ despite the awful trials they had to suffer. In this sense Blandina as a mother brought her children to life. And as a good mother she shared in her children's suffering:

> But the blessed Blandina, last of all, like a noble mother who has encouraged her children and sent them forth triumphant to the king, herself also enduring all the conflicts of the children, hastened to them, rejoicing and glad at her departure as if called to a marriage feast and not being thrown to the beasts.[18]

Blandina is a living sign of the Church's own reality. Blandina brought all of God's children safely to Christ, which was precisely the desire of Virgin Mother Church described earlier by Eusebius. Mother Church experienced great anxiety that not all her children

---

17. Eusebius' chief source is the "Epistle of the Church of Vienne and Lyons" which contains the acts of the martyrs persecuted in this region. The *Fathers of the Church*, Vol. 19, p. 273 has a detailed footnote regarding this letter which states that the letter "bears all the marks of authenticity and its genuineness has never been questioned."

18. Eusebius, *Ecclesiastical History*, 5, 1, trans. Roy J. Deferrari, *The Fathers of the Church*, Vol. 19 (New York: Fathers of the Church, Inc., 1953), 282 (PG 20.425–426).

would be born. In other words, that some would deny Christ and thus be stillborn from her.

> Through the living the dead were made alive, and martyrs gave grace to those who failed to be martyrs, and there was great joy in the Virgin Mother, as she received back alive those who had been brought forth as dead. For, through them, most of those who had denied were restored [to their Mother] again and were conceived again and were made alive again and learned to confess; now alive and strong, as God made them happy, who desires not the death of the sinner but is kind towards repentance. . . . [19]

In her own life Blandina expresses the reality of Mother Church, causing those children of the Church who fail in the faith to be "conceived again" and made "alive again."

Blandina's prototype exists in the mother of the Maccabees. This valiant woman of the Old Testament is the primary religious teacher and source of courage for her seven sons. She exercises her maternal authority in leading her sons to martyrdom for the sake of God's law. When all but one has yet to suffer cruel torture and be put to death, the pagan king Antiochus hopes to win this youngest son away from the Hebrew faith. He entices him with promises of riches and power, but the boy's mother instructs him to be strong and appeals to him precisely from her maternal authority, as she with God is his source of life (2 Mac 7:22–23).

> But, leaning close to him, she spoke in their native tongue as follows, deriding the cruel tyrant: "My son, have pity on me. I carried you nine months in my womb, and nursed you for three years, and have reared you and brought you up to this point in your life, and have taken care of you. I beg you,

---

19. Ibid., 285 (PG 20.431–432).

my child, to look at the heaven and the earth and see everything that is in them, and recognize that God did not make
them out of things that existed. Thus also mankind comes
into being. Do not fear this butcher, but prove worthy of
your brothers. Accept death, so that in God's mercy I may
get you back again with your brothers." (2 Mac 7:27–29)

If the mother of the Maccabees is the prototype of Blandina, she
is also the prototype of Mary. The mother of seven sons aids each of
them in achieving their ultimate destiny, as did the mother of Christ.
The death of the seventh son is even described as a saving sacrifice:
"I, like my brothers, give up body and life for the laws of our fathers,
appealing to God to show mercy soon to our nation and by afflictions
and plagues to make you confess that he alone is God, and through
me and my brothers to bring to an end the wrath of the Almighty
which has justly fallen on our whole nation" (2 Mac 37–38).

After the death of her last son the mother too was finally killed.
The actions of the Maccabees' mother is repeated in Blandina, who
after encouraging her children to be true to the Lord, in the end
shared in their suffering.

THE MOTHER OF AUGUSTINE

St. Monica is a good example of a woman who personified the maternal authority of the Church. St. Augustine himself credits Monica with his own conversion to the Catholic faith by her example,
prayers, admonitions, and pious sacrifices. In *Confessions*, Augustine
writes: "Out of the blood of my mother's heart, through the tears she
poured out day and night, a sacrifice was offered up to you in my
behalf, and you dealt with me in a wondrous way."[20] In another passage, Augustine compares his mother's tears to the waters of Baptism

---

20. St. Augustine, *Confessions*, 5, 7, 13, trans. R.S. Pine-Coffin (New York:
Penguin Books, 1961), 99 (CSEL 33.99–100).

through which Augustine would later be reborn. Addressing God, Augustine states: "You preserved me all full of execrable filth, from the waters of the sea and kept me safe for the waters of your grace. For when I would be washed clean by that water, then also would be dried up those rivers flowing down my mother's eyes, by which before you and in my behalf, she daily watered the ground beneath her face."[21]

Monica's influence over her son, and especially her prayers, are the source of Augustine's rebirth in the waters of Baptism. Monica is not only her son's natural mother, but also his spiritual mother. "I have no words," states Augustine, "to express the love she had for me, and with how much more anguish she was now suffering the pangs of childbirth for my spiritual state than when she had given birth to me physically."[22] Augustine frequently spoke of the Church as a mother giving birth to her children through the baptismal font. Certainly, the powerful role Monica played in his spiritual development shaped his theology of the Church.

There is a stern and harsh motherhood in Monica that reflects a truth about the Church's own maternity. The Church as the Bride of Christ and the mother of God's children being "without spot or wrinkle" refuses to be tainted with corrupt doctrine. When Augustine became a Manichean, Monica shut him out of her house and excommunicated him from her presence because he embraced heresy. As long as he continued in this error the son was no longer a part of her household. The mother of Augustine is for him what the Mater Ecclesia is for all those who choose to be separated from her. The Church is not only gentle, but terrible. She demands that souls steeped in error realize the seriousness of their sins and return to her heart. De Lubac comments:

---

21. Ibid., 5, 8, 15, p. 101 (CSEL 33.101).
22. Ibid., 5, 9, 15, p. 102 (CSEL 33.103).

A truly loving mother, she saved our personal life, not by flattering our instincts, but by calling us back to both the gentleness and strictness of the Gospel. We must place ourselves, not on the psychological level, but on the spiritual ("pneumatic") level in order to judge this. It is at the moment when her countenance seems perhaps austere to us that she is best fulfilling her maternal function.[23]

Monica only consents to live with Augustine after she has a dream about his conversion. In the dream, Monica laments for her son's perdition, but a young man in the dream reassures her "that she should attend and see that where she was, there was I also." The "I" being her son Augustine. Monica is standing on a wooden measuring rod that is a symbol for the "rule of faith."[24] The dream gives Monica great comfort. Through it she was able to see in her son the future son of the Church, and thus, while Augustine was still a Manichean, Monica was able to "share the same table" with him in his home.

Not only did Monica bring Augustine into the Church but she was also responsible for converting her pagan husband Patricius. Just before he died he consented to be baptized. In this way Monica triumphed over Patricius's infidelity to her by bringing him to God. Augustine shows great respect for Monica in the conversion of his father, and she is cherished and loved by Augustine as someone who gave life to him and to others.

She had brought up her children and had been in travail afresh each time she saw them go astray from you. Finally, O Lord, since by your gift you allow us to speak as your servants, she took care of us all when we received the grace of your baptism and were living as companions before she

---

23. Henri de Lubac, *Motherhood of the Church* (San Francisco: Ignatius Press, 1982), 159.

24. St. Augustine, *Confessions*, 3, 11, 5, p. 68 (CSEL 33.61).

fell asleep in you. She took good care of us, as though she had been the mother of us all. . . . [25]

The words "She took care of us all when we received the grace of your baptism" shows that Monica was a living expression of the Church. Monica is the center of Augustine's post-baptismal life and her role is not just to look after his physical needs. She is Augustine's spiritual guide. She astonishes him and his companions with the depth of her contempt for this life, and with her spiritual courage in the face of death of which they didn't think a woman capable.[26]

St. Monica's final request before she died was to be remembered at the altar during the sacrifice of the Eucharist. We can be quite sure that Augustine, the priest, did not fail to fulfill his mother's request. In this we see the drama of Mother Church, who Augustine himself called the mother of her fathers. This motherhood of the Church was accomplished in Monica. Monica is the spiritual mother of her son and so led him to his fatherhood, which he then exercised on her behalf and on behalf of the whole Mother Church from whom he was born.

ST. CATHERINE—THE POPE'S GUIDE

The fourteenth century provides us with a paradigm of the Church as mother through the life and work of St. Catherine of Siena. Her entire life exudes authority as Catherine, in her maternal role, acts to bring restoration to a Church marred by confusion, disunity, and corruption. Catherine is a teacher, preacher, reformer, and envoy of Christ, whose God-given vocation was to mediate between Christ and the pope, and between the pope and the faithful. She called men back to the pure love of Christ. Often her message was directed

---

25. Ibid., 9, 9, 15, p. 196 (CSEL 33.215).
26. Ibid., 9, 11, 20, p. 200 (CSEL 33.219).

at bishops with the intention of reforming those who represent the headship of Christ.

> In a letter to the bishop of Florence, Angelo Ricasoli, surrounded by numerous prelates immersed in politics and worldly affairs, Catherine recalls the obligations of charity and of courage in the ministry, the duty of conferring spiritual and temporal goods for the good of the brethren . . . not engaging in financial speculations, not squandering in riotous living the patrimony of the Church, which belongs to the poor, but rather honoring God and serving their brethren. This is the job of pastors![27]

Catherine is almost singlehandedly responsible for the return of the papacy to Rome after its seventy year exile in Avignon, France. She alone instilled in Pope Gregory the necessary courage to make the move.

> With words of fire, now more than ever convinced that she speaks with the will of God, Catherine breaks the Pope's indecision and—alone—defeats the whole crowd of opposition, representing the top leaders of the Church and in the Papal states.[28]

Later in the struggle between Pope Urban VI and the antipope Clement VII, Catherine valiantly rises to the defense of the true papacy.

> It is she who gives the Pope courage, who reminds him of the high dignity of his office and exhorts him to take up again the tradition of irreproach which had always characterized the Vicars of Christ, surrounding himself with

27. Igino Giordini, *Catherine of Siena, Fire and Blood* (Milwaukee: Bruce Publishing Co., 1959), 137.
28. Ibid., 179.

counselors and functionaries of unsustained lives, now that he was freed of trafficers in blood. Only Catherine would dare to advance this sort of advice, to make suggestions to the Pope . . . Pope Urban . . . was the target of all sorts of threats from kings and powerful rulers; but he did have on his side a pure and invincible power: Catherine of Siena.[29]

Catherine not only gives courage to Urban VI but she severely reproaches those Italian cardinals who dared to rise up against him. The election of the antipope seized her with a just rage and impelled her to write to three Italian cardinals. She did not even hesitate to call these men of ecclesial rank blind liars and idolaters![30] Catherine images the Church as teacher, who is desperately trying to restore order among her children. Her children include not only the simple faithful and priests, but bishops, cardinals, and even the pope. Note that in her own feminine authority she does not attempt to take over the authority of the priests or that of the pope; rather, her authority is exercised precisely to enable the pope to be pope! Catherine continues the role of Mary at Cana. Mary provoked Christ to His public life—to His salvific mission. Catherine provokes and exhorts Christ's vicar on earth to fulfill his mission as head of the Church.

ST. MARGARET CLITHEROW

On March 25, 1586, St. Margaret Clitherow of York was martyred for the Catholic faith during the reign of Queen Elizabeth I. Alongside Edmund Campion, John Fisher, and Robert Southwell, this woman's extraordinary life and death contributed to the survival of the Catholic Church in England during the second half of the English Reformation.

---

29. Ibid., 182.
30. Ibid., 218.

Margaret converted to Catholicism at a time when being a faithful Catholic meant definite persecution and possible death. She is a true mother of the Church and bride of Christ. This is seen, for example, when she took the necessary risks to see to it that her children were given a proper religious education. Margaret had hired a Catholic tutor, Brian Stapleton, who had already proved his fidelity to Christ as he had spent several years in prison. Margaret hid Stapleton in her home where he catechized her children.

Not only was Margaret concerned for her children's learning, but she was also extremely solicitous about her husband's spiritual well-being. A biography about Margaret states: "The problem of her husband touched her at every level."[31] According to her marriage vows she had promised to obey John, but when it came to God's affairs Margaret exercised feminine authority over him so as to bring his soul to salvation.

> John was a human soul in danger of damnation, "one of those with whom she might safely deal" in discussing religion, a soul entrusted to her just as much as her children were, and to him she felt the same responsibility for instruction and conversion.[32]

In her own life, Margaret made real the maternity of the Church by her zeal and heartfelt concern for the conversion of souls. Her greatest anguish was the terrible loss of souls through apostasy and the attack upon the Church's unity that such apostasy caused. Her life is a continuation of the martyrs of Vienne and Lyon, who spoke of the sorrow of the Virgin Mother whenever her children gave up the faith of Christ.[33]

---

31. Katherine M. Longley, *St. Margaret Clitherow* (Wheathampsted-Hertfordshire, England: Anthony Clarke, 1986), 99.

32. Ibid.

33. Ibid., 90.

Margaret was murdered by the English government for the "crime" of harboring a priest in her own home, Fr. Mush. Her desire to hide him was motivated by a love for the Eucharist, so that the worship of the Church might continue. Again, in this act Margaret most clearly exemplifies the maternal nature of the Church. By this act, Margaret made her own home an ecclesia wherein the priesthood of Christ could function and have its place as it functions in the universal Mater Ecclesia. While calling Margaret his "virtuous daughter," Fr. Mush also referred to her as his "blessed mother."[34]

Margaret's maternal authority can be credited with her daughter entering religious life. Margaret even sent her son, Henry, to France to educate him for the priesthood (though he was never ordained) and did so without the knowledge of her husband. Separation from her son was a truly heroic act as he was only twelve years old, and if he had been ordained he could only have exercised the priesthood in England under considerable danger. But Margaret behaved toward Henry as Mary did toward Christ. As life-givers to their sons they had to experience a separation, but it is a parting they initiated that enabled their sons to walk the path of God.

In the giving up of her children, Margaret shared in "the hour" of Mary. Margaret died a martyr, but the one thing that would have caused her to deny the faith and spare her execution was the love she felt so deeply for her children and her keen sense of motherly duty toward them.

> She had . . . offered her son Henry freely to God when she
> sent him abroad, and she well knew that her children's con-
> stancy in the Faith depended on her own. . . . If ever a
> woman loved her children in Christ it was this one, and two
> at least did their utmost to follow the example of her life. It
> had been the will of God that she should bear them; now

---

34. Ibid., 87.

he had expressed his will in another way. He had an even higher task for her than their upbringing: to die for him.[35]

Margaret understood her own martyrdom as a ceremony in which she would be wedded to Christ. In martyrdom she is *in persona ecclesia*, a living sign of the Church's own reality. In Margaret's response to Christ, the response of the Church is made manifest to the world. Margaret deliberately planned to die in a white linen smock, which was her wedding gown.

> She occupied herself in these last days with an important piece of needlework. She must have asked Mrs. Vavasour to obtain a piece of linen for her . . . and with it she had always been "quick in the dispatch of business" made "a linen habit like an alb . . . to suffer martyrdom in."
>
> Margaret has two purposes in view in making this garment; one was symbolic, for her mind at this time dealt in symbols. The making of this white garment reveals her heart more clearly than words can say. Another Yorkshire martyr, the great St. John Fisher, had taken the same action fifty years earlier. On the morning of his execution he asked his manservant "to lay him out a clean white shirt, and all the best apparel he had as cleanly brushed as might be," and to his enquiry replied, "Dost thou not mark that this is our marriage day, and that it behooveth us therefore to use more cleanliness for solemnity of that marriage?"
>
> It is the symbolism of the Apocalypse: "For the marriage of the Lamb is come: and the wife hath prepared herself. And it is granted to her that she should clothe herself with fine linen, glittering and white. For the white linen is the justification of the saints. And he said to me: 'Write:

---

35. Ibid., 151–2.

Blessed are they who are called to the marriage supper of the Lamb'" (Apoc 19: 7–9). [36]

What St. John Fisher was by imitation, St. Margaret Clitherow, by virtue of her sex, was in reality: the covenant partner of Christ as bridal Church. Her biographer says of Margaret: "It was as a bride that she stepped out of the New Counter prison."[37]

MODERN CHURCH MOTHERS

Our own time is full of instances of feminine ecclesial authority. One major way feminine authority is exercised is through the female leaders of the Right to Life movement in the United States and Europe. Women are active and involved on every level of this struggle from founding and operating pregnancy help centers, serving the movement as attorneys, involvement in politics, activism of every kind, and educational efforts. It is worth noting that it is women, namely Linda Gibbons and Mary Wagner, who are performing some of the most significant acts of sacrificial love in reaching out to women and their unborn children at Canadian abortion clinics and paying a heavy price in long jail terms for doing so.

The story of Adele Nathanson provides us with a true and powerful instance of feminine authority. In the middle and late 1960s, her husband, Bernard Nathanson, was a key promoter of legalized abortion in the United States. A gynecologist/obstetrician, he directed the busiest abortion clinic in the world in New York City when the state of New York legalized abortion through the sixth month of pregnancy. In November 1974, Nathanson shocked the pro-abortion community when in the *New England Journal of Medicine* he publicly confessed that he was responsible for killing over sixty thousand human lives by abortion. That was the beginning of a moral and

36. Ibid., 154–5.
37. Ibid., 156.

spiritual trek that would eventually bring Nathanson from avowed atheism to baptism in the Catholic Church. In his book *Aborting America*, Nathanson credited his new found respect for human life to his having become acquainted with the science of fetology. He insisted over and over again that pure science alone caused his dramatic moral shift, but there was far more to his conversion than pure "objective" science could offer. Science may be able to determine whether the unborn are human, but it cannot determine the value to be placed upon human life. Thus Nathanson's change could not simply be the result of having attained more information. His change was an alternation of his moral view of the world.

The making of an abortionist who killed over sixty thousand human beings into one of the most articulate, intelligent, and tireless champions of the unborn child's right to life is the result of his wife Adele's moral instruction to him in the years preceding his public confession. Adele Nathanson herself revealed this fact during a speech she delivered May 1, 1988, at an Operation Rescue rally in New York City. She exercised an authority over her husband. She called her husband to be a righteous man, and did so completely in keeping with everything the Fathers of the Church have to say on the subject of a woman's rights over her husband. Adele spoke of her long, difficult, and painful ministry to Bernard in order to call him away from evil. One can say that Bernard Nathanson's conversion was not caused by his fidelity to pure science, but by his wife's pure fidelity to him.

THE AUTHORITY OF JOAN ANDREWS BELL

When we seek modern examples of feminine authority we must stop and ponder the life of Joan Andrews Bell. She is one of the most powerful women in the Right to Life movement although she has neither founded a pro-life organization nor holds any official position within the movement. Her power is, again, not one of office in the formal sense of that word, but flows directly from her womanly faithfulness to God and His creation, by which she is a true mother. She is a true mother because of her uncompromising sacrifices for the outcast children of other mothers who seek to undo their lives in the coldness and alienation of the abortion chamber

In March 1986, Joan Andrews entered a Pensacola, Florida abortion center and attempted to pull from its wall socket the plug of a suction machine used to kill unborn children. She was charged with burglary, malicious mischief, resisting arrest, and assault. She refused to promise not to engage in even legal actions to save the unborn from abortion. To her, such a promise was scandalous. The assault charges, which in Florida carry a life sentence, were dropped because they were false.[38]

She was convicted in a non-jury trial before Judge William Anderson. Because of her "non-repentant" attitude, refusing to promise to cease her "illegal" defense of unborn children in the future, Anderson, on September 24, 1986, sentenced Joan to a five-year prison term. Her sentence was far beyond the Florida sentencing guidelines that recommended a year to thirty months maximum for convicted burglars.[39]

In prison Joan refused to cooperate with the system because she believed God called her to witness for the unborn. That conviction required of her a firm resolve not to give in to anything designed to assert her guilt for having tried to protect His children.[40] Her motherhood took her to the Broward Correctional Institute, which houses Florida's most dangerous female criminals, where she spent twenty-one months in solitary confinement.

38. Richard Cowden Guido, *You Reject Them, You Reject Me: The Prison Letters of Joan Andrews* (Manassas, VA: Trinity Communications, 1988), 16.

39. Ibid., 17.

40. Ibid., 172.

Because of her courage and love, Joan inspired hundreds of others to understand pro-life work not simply on the level of political strategy, but on the level of spiritual sacrifice in which the pro-lifer erases all distinctions between himself and the unwanted unborn child.[41] In this sacrificial love of the Cross, God's graces multiplied.

The authority of Joan is the covenantal authority of Mary who offered herself with her Son at the foot of the Cross. In a letter written from prison addressed to all those who wrote to her or who prayed for her during her incarceration, Joan states:

> Could I ask something more of you—something far more important than any aid you could ever give me directly or materially, but which would benefit me and yourselves, our Holy Faith, the nation, and all people beyond any ability to estimate? Would you spend some time with the little babies in your own neighborhood before they die? Maybe you'll be able to directly save some lives, maybe not. What's more important, you'll be there. In a sense it may be a way to redeem the abandonment of Jesus by His apostles, when they refused to be with Him at His death—too often, we refuse to be with Jesus for fear of the Cross, do we not? These little ones dying today are directly connected with the sufferings and the death of Our Savior. There is a bond here that must not be overlooked. All the political action, educating, donation of funds, demonstrations, alternative work, important and necessary as these are, do not make up for an absence at the death scene. Thus let me beg you to view your presence at the killing center in your area as the place where God wants you to be. Grab your rosary, pick up your Bible, bring your devotionals, and go out to the Calvary not far from you—where Christ is being crucified today in your midst.[42]

41. Ibid., 21.
42. Ibid., 219.

The New Testament tells a story about Mary and Christ's brothers who come to see Him (Mt 12:46–50). When Jesus hears that they are outside He responds:

> "Who is my mother, and who are my brethren?" And stretching out his hand toward his disciples, he said, "Here are my mother and my brethren! For whoever does the will of my Father in heaven is my brother, and sister, and mother." (Mt 12:48b–50)

Mary was never more the mother of Christ than when she stood with Him on Calvary. A woman mothers Christ when she becomes, like Mary, the covenantal partner of redemption, when she exercises motherhood toward those who suffer, particularly when this entails becoming poor and outcast herself. Replicated in her life is the maternal solicitude of the Church in union with the sacrificed Son of God.

A well-known pro-life leader tried to persuade Joan that she should try and get out of prison as soon as possible because he believed being in jail was of no practical service to the pro-life movement. Joan shunned the "practical" strategist's way of doing things precisely to illustrate that the value of human beings was something that could not be compromised. She stated:

> The world always wants to slaughter the Jews or Arabs, or the bourgeoisie, or "uppity" blacks, or the preborn children, or the "unfit" as Margaret Sanger considered them to be and her Planned Parenthood still does—as a practical measure to make things easier on a more privileged group of people. And it has always been the Church, sometimes more bravely, sometimes less, that has stood in the path of this "practical" approach. . . . I think it may be true that the world in a particular way needs the Church—needs Christians—to be especially brave today, in order to rescue the world once

again from its maniacal understanding of "practicality."
Needs this more than even the shrewdest practical calculation . . . I do believe that faithfulness is . . . the shrewdest
practical political calculation.[43]

Joan, from an exercise of her own motherhood to Christ and
to the literally outcast unborn children, articulates the motherhood
of the Church who, in this age when human beings everywhere are
sacrificed to what is practical and utilitarian, stands up to protect
the inherent, God-given dignity of each person. This kind of defense
comes from the nature of motherhood.

The woman is the force in the world who stands as the bulwark
against everything in this utilitarian era that threatens to reduce the
person to a thing.[44] A woman knows she has given birth to a man,
not a thing, whose life has been entrusted to her protection in a special way. She knows that the bond between her and the life she has
created cannot be reduced to serving mere practical societal goals.

The authority of Joan Andrews Bell is clearly seen from the fact
that her example helped cause Auxiliary Bishop Austin Vaughn of
the New York archdiocese to join in the pro-life rescue movement
and himself risk arrest and jail. In a May 1, 1988 speech, Vaughn
publicly credited Joan with showing him the value of her type of sacrifice for life. We see here the authority of a woman who called a head
of the Church to give deeper witness to the truth of Christ's Church,
and called him to a purer exercise of his own fatherhood in Christ.

43. Ibid., 177.

44. Karl Stern, *The Flight From Woman* (New York: Paragon House, 1965), 268.
According to Stern it is a masculine tendency to appreciate the human being on
the level of what is practical. He gives a critique of the character Raskolnikov from
Dostoievsky's novel *Crime and Punishment*. The character murders a man for whom he
sees no value. Stern calls this "Life seen in terms of logistics—this is sheer maleness,
unfettered and crazed."

WOMEN AND OFFICE

As we have seen, it is a mistake to confuse authority with the holding of formal office. Authority is not synonymous with power. Authority is not power as quantified strength so that one's personal will may be accomplished. Still, it is pertinent to ask: is it consistent with the meaning of feminine authority for women to occupy certain offices within the Church? It is not possible for women to be priests since their sacramental function is to be the sign of the Church in relation to Christ, but there are other formal ecclesial positions women may be able to occupy where feminine authority can be exercised. For example, women can and do teach at seminaries. The education of priests need not necessarily be in the hands of men only, or of priests only. A female theology professor can be a very valuable asset to a seminary faculty. A female teacher who is devoted to the faith of the Church and seeks to inspire future priests with that same devotion, while at the same time deepening their intellectual grasp of that faith, may be a far better educator of priests than a man who has difficulty accepting the faith or is more interested in promoting theological confusion at the seminary level. We must keep in mind that a woman teacher exercises authority according to her uniquely feminine life-giving powers. A female seminary professor can help future priests appreciate, respect, and even obey women who desire to lead them to God.

Feminine authority can also be exercised through the various appointments and offices of a diocesan chancery. Delores Greer, for example, served as vice-chancellor for John Cardinal O'Connor of New York. Delores was an African-American convert to Catholicism and a single woman, and even though she occupied this high profile position she was not an advocate of the ordination of women. A woman in her position has a unique opportunity to work for the faith of the Church and be a witness to the Church's truth about women. Working in a chancery post is not simply a job. It is an apostolate. A female diocesan chancellor works for the sake of her bishop and for the good of the souls under his care. There are several diocesan positions that women can fill, such as heading up the Office for Worship, the Office for Catholic Education, as well as family, pro-life, and natural family planning apostolates, catechetics, and retreat work. Women religious can appropriately be in charge of offices that oversee the organization of women's religious orders in a diocese and manage projects that have to do directly with the affairs of nuns and sisters, even to the point of being the bishop's aide and intermediary in conflicts, disputes, and discipline. Furthermore, nothing sacramentally stands in the way of a bishop having a woman serve as his chief theological advisor, although usually such appointments are filled by priest theologians.

WOMEN AS CARDINALS

The question has been raised: is it possible for women to be cardinals? Since the cardinalate is not a part of Holy Orders, what then stands in the way of women being raised to the status of cardinal?

Perhaps a more fundamental question needs to be asked: what would be the point of making women cardinals? First of all, it would have the effect of appeasing some feminists. I say some, not all. In fact, the most hardcore feminists would not at all be satisfied with such a move since they would undoubtedly see this as participation in an institution inherently tied to the patriarchal Church, and any woman made a cardinal would still have been granted this position from the male dominated hierarchy. For feminists, the cardinalate is seen as part and parcel of the male hierarchy, and nothing would be solved as long as that hierarchy still exists, because women cardinals would be mere token minority figures in an all-male club.

Secondly, if women were cardinals their sphere of influence might be expanded since, after all, cardinals are publicly known and accorded respect. Some bishops are raised to the College of Cardinals due to the size of their diocese. Priests are sometimes accorded this honor in recognition of service to the Church. Theologians such as John Henry Newman, Henri de Lubac, and Hans Urs Von Balthazar were given this honor.

When Rembert Weakland was archbishop of Milwaukee, he spoke in favor of giving women leadership positions within the Vatican curia. In a column he wrote for the *New York Times* (Dec. 6, 1992), Weakland said that "[F]or much of its history the Roman Catholic Church has assumed that women are inferior to men." He claimed this injustice is buttressed by the Church's "exclusion of women from the priesthood." He believed the Church must set an example to the world that women are equal to men. Church law must be reformed so that jurisdictional authority and power is no longer tied to the priesthood "so that women can take on active roles on all levels," meaning that women "must be integrated at the Vatican itself." The Vatican has diplomatic relations with one hundred and thirty countries. Weakland believes that women can be Vatican diplomats instead of filling these positions with archbishops who use monsignors as their aides.

The late Cardinal John O'Connor, archbishop of New York, published a response to Weakland in his diocesan paper *Catholic New York* (Dec. 10, 1992). He questioned whether female diplomats would be accepted in every country and, on this level, thought their appointment to these posts impractical. This, however, does not go to the heart of the matter. O'Connor raises a more pertinent point. Vatican posts are part of the hierarchical structure of the Church. It is hierarchical because it is apostolic. He is concerned that the hierarchical structure of the Church would be damaged if women were admitted to Vatican posts. The diplomatic corps of the Vatican is an extension of the apostolic nature of the Church. Christ appointed the Apostles as his representatives, thus there is a certain sacramental appropriateness that Vatican diplomats participate in the ministerial priesthood of the Church. This sacramental appropriateness is similar to the liturgical appropriateness of male altar servers. Of course, on a purely functional level, girls and women can perform the duties of altar server; nevertheless, there is a certain sacramental appropriateness that altar servers be male. The priest stands *in persona Christi*. This sacramental reality is most explicitly expressed when the priest offers the sacrifice of Christ's Body and Blood as Bridegroom to the Church. Liturgically, an altar server is an extension of the male priest's position on the altar. Female altar servers blur the necessarily masculine liturgical character of the priest. The actions of the sanctuary are on the side of Christ, who speaks His nuptial love for the Church. In the same way, Vatican diplomats are an extension of the apostolic office of the Church. Yes, women can serve in this capacity, but doing so lacks the sacramental appropriateness of the office.[45]

I think it is possible for women to serve in the Vatican curia, perhaps even as heads of various offices, especially those having to do with spirituality and women's religious orders. Women ought to be sought as theological and pastoral advisors within the Vatican. I am sympathetic to the idea of appointing women cardinals because I would like to see women of rare devotion be recognized in an institutionally formal way for the enrichment of the Church. But such an appointment would have to be merely for the purposes of conferring a title of honor to women who have rendered some kind of outstanding service to the Church. Lady cardinals would not be able to vote for the pope as part of the College of Cardinals. It seems to

---

45. Joseph Fessio, "Reasons Given Against Women Acolytes and Lectors," *Origins*, 17 (Nov. 12, 1987), 397–9. An argument against female altar servers can also be applied in the case of women serving in the role of cardinal. The altar server is the assistant of the priest acting *in persona Christi* and therefore a true liturgical appropriateness exists in male altar servers. The altar server is an extension of the priest and aids the priest in his sacramental role which is inherently masculine. This sort of male appropriateness is also pertinent to the position of cardinal and curial leadership.

me that this privilege is tied to apostolic office, as bishops have been entrusted with governing the Church and women cannot be bishops.

The ecclesiological problem with making women cardinals is the one O'Connor pointed out with women serving in top Vatican posts. The position of cardinal is part of the hierarchy of the Church. Cardinals were often pastors of important churches, particularly in Rome. From the eleventh century to the present time they acted as assistants and special counselors to the pope. However, prior to the 1917 Code of Canon Law, the title of cardinal could be conferred on a layman. This fact leads us to inquire whether it is possible for women to be granted this honor. Working in the Vatican is not necessarily tied to hierarchical office, but the position of cardinal from its inception has been linked to apostolic office. Newman, De Lubac, and Von Balthasar were at least priests. On the practical and symbolic level, a cardinal is a magnification of the pope's presence. They work for him and speak for him in his own formal apostolate as successor to St. Peter. For this reason it would probably not be appropriate for women to be made cardinals, though not all cardinals are so intimately allied with the papal office. Nonetheless, the desire for lady cardinals suffers in many ways from the same theological errors underlying the push for women priests. It is a mistake to believe that for women to be equal they must have what men have or be what men are. If authority is shut up inside of a monist, radically singular God who is not in relation with his creation and whose authority is not exercised covenantally, then certainly, women must "get themselves up into God" to ensure their equality with men. In other words, women must make sure the deity is equally reflective of males and females—or contains within "itself" masculinity and femininity—in the sense that women mistakenly believe that their worth is determined by "getting femininity" up into God. But this is not the covenantal order of authority upon which the Christian religion is based.

SOME FINAL WORDS

The authority of women in the Catholic Church could be illuminated by examining the lives of St. Joan of Arc, Mother Seton, Dorothy Day, Mother Cabrini, and Sr. Irene McCormick who died at the hands of Peruvian terrorists, including a host of other Christian women, both ancient and contemporary. Also undoubtedly pertinent are the millions of Christian women who are not famous or known in any way, but whose domestic authority is the concrete spiritual backbone of the covenant of salvation as it must be made real in the world today until the return of the Lord.

It is clear that authority, whether male or female, cannot be reduced to sheer possession of power for the sake of dominating the direction or order of the group. Authority is not extrinsic organizational force. The authority of the covenant of redemption is certainly not this. When we talk about the authority of Christ, the Head, and His Bride, the Church, we are really speaking at the edge of a mystery. Covenantal authority is the basis of creation and redemption and must be lived as a mystery—a living and an understanding that is only truly possible through grace.

The greatest spiritual danger for the Church that will collapse her covenantal authority is the desire of women to either destroy or possess what the man has. When women do this, they deny and forfeit their own dignity and responsibility. This is, of course, the essence of the push for female priests. For the woman to own what the man has will not result in simply exercising an authority that has been "reserved" to him, because to destroy this authority is to destroy him. Karl Stern gives us a picture of this kind of destruction and what is at its roots in his examination of Ibsen's character Hedda Gabler, from the play of the same name.

> Women like Hedda seem not to be created for the polarity of love. They waiver between either pole. They are of-

ten attracted to sensitive men like Lovborg. Most of George Sand's lovers were Ejlert Lovborgs. The artist's soul is a lock to which the woman wants to be key—and to be key, not lock, is the leading phantasy of her life. But whether she plays at key or lock she can never fit because she lacks complementariness. The only form of union of which her feelings are capable is not the union of love but the union of "power over," of ownership.[46]

If we look at Mary we see that the mystery of feminine authority lies not in the Prometheian lust to take power for oneself, but precisely in the power to receive and to be filled; to be the absolute antithesis of the modern curse of man's refusal to receive help from above.[47]

In the above quotation Stern hits upon a fundamental basis for male and female authority, namely the order of complementarity. The first thing that must go is the idea that authority has to do with competition between beings who are different. Stern comments:

Only complementariness can make us self-less. This self can only be lost in the other, in something which is not self. It is complementariness which mobilizes our generosity. Hence the phallic woman who denies otherness cannot love. All she can do is compete, and this often in an illusory way. If the male partner is weaker, things don't work out because he is weaker. If he is stronger, they don't work because he is stronger. He cannot win, neither can she. In the first case it is disdain that prevents her from loving, in the second it is envy. . . . She cannot be helpmate. . . . It is a beautiful expression, and it pertains equally to man and woman. For just as woman for her greatest creative act needs to conceive

---

46. Stern, *Flight*, 154–5.
47. Ibid., 270.

from the male, man, for his creative activity, is in need of a
mysterious "conception" from the female.[48]

Authority is connected to being an origin, a source of life, and to
appreciate the meaning of covenantal authority is never to go astray
from the words of St. Paul: "Nevertheless, in the Lord woman is not
independent of man nor man of woman; for as woman was made
from man, so man is now born of woman. And all things are from
God" (1 Cor 11:11–12).

The very order of redemption is bound to this interdependency
and mystery of the sexes. Scripture attests that woman is the place
where God dwells, the New Jerusalem come down from heaven,
beautiful as a bride: "The dwelling of God is with men" (Rev 21:3).
The covenant rests within this mystery of sexual unity. God saves
the world through His relation to the Church. Of this relation Scripture testifies, "He will dwell with them, and they shall be his people,
and God himself will be with them" (Rev 21:3b). In this covenant it
is the authority of the woman who holds the Almighty One to the
earth. The Scriptures say, "Come, I will show you the Bride, the wife
of the Lamb" (Rev 21:9c). When there is neither death, nor mourn-
ing, and the "former world has passed away," woman will still reveal
the splendor of the Church.

---

48. Ibid., 146–7.

QUEEN MOTHER

EDWARD SRI

– General Editor –

SCOTT HAHN

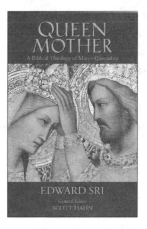

Queen Mother explores the role of the queen mother in the Davidic kingdom, examining the ways in which this theme sheds light on Mary's role as heavenly Queen and Mother of the Church. As he proceeds through the New Testament, Dr. Sri demonstrates the ultimate convergence of the queen-mother theme in the Gospels and the Book of Revelation.

978-1-931018-24-1 // paperback
978-1-63446-018-7 // hardbound

....

"The biblical queen-mother tradition is of paramount importance for our contemporary understanding of Our Lady's dynamic role of spiritual queen and advocate for all humanity. Edward Sri offers an outstanding synthesis of this *Gebirah* or 'Great Lady' biblical revelation."

—MARK MIRAVALLE, S.T.D. Professor of Theology,
Franciscan University of Steubenville

"This book intelligently deepens one's devotion to Mary, the Queen of Heaven, the Mother of Jesus, and the Mother of the Church."

—REV. JOSEPH HENCHEY, C.S.S. Professor Emeritus,
Pontifical North American College, Rome

emmausroad.org • (800) 398-5470

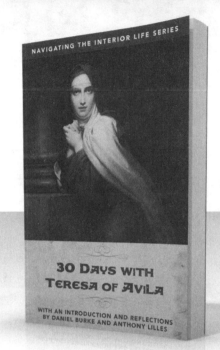

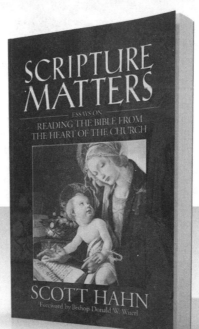